# Gender & Culture

# Gender & Culture
## Kibbutz Women Revisited

# Melford E. Spiro

**With a New Introduction by the Author**

## Transaction Publishers
**New Brunswick (U.S.A.) and London (U.K.)**

Library of Congress Catalog Number: 95-20370
ISBN: 1-56000-771-0
Printed in the United States of America

Library of Congress Cataloging-in-Publication Data

Spiro, Melford E.
    Gender and culture : kibbutz women revisited / Melford E. Spiro, with a new introduction by the author.
        p.  cm.
    Includes bibliographical references and index.
    ISBN 1-56000-771-0 (pbk. : alk. paper)
    1. Kibbutzim.  2. Women—Israel.  I. Title.
HX742.2.A3S64  1995
307.77'6'082—dc20                                                  95-20370
                                                                          CIP

To Audrey

# Contents

# Introduction to the Transaction edition

## On the sociology of knowledge

Although first published in 1979, this study of women and gender in the Israeli kibbutz movement has the dubious distinction of having virtually never been cited or referenced in the veritable library of books, articles, collections, bibliographies, and review articles dealing with the comparative study of women and gender published since then. This distinction, however, is both unfortunate and anomalous.

It is unfortunate because the kibbutz story told here raises critical issues that are at the core of current debates regarding gender and gender differences—their origin and development, their relationship to sex and sex differences, the relative importance of biological, cultural, and experiential determinants, and so forth—but since this story is unknown, it has not contributed to these debates.

This distinction is also anomalous because as a rare longitudinal study—it is based on historical documentation of some seventy years, and ethnographic observations extending over twenty-five—its findings are arguably no less important, and their theoretical implications no less significant, than the findings of other comparative studies of women and gender that have become part of the scientific record. Moreover, that a somewhat earlier study of kibbutz women with virtually identical findings (Tiger and Shepher 1975) has had the same history as this one makes the anomaly all the more problematic.

Admittedly, this anomaly may be more apparent than real: many studies of potential theoretical significance are nevertheless ignored because their scholarship is defective. This, however, does not seem to be true of this study (nor that of Tiger and Shepher), for while most of the reviewers of this book were highly critical of its interpretations, none of them, however, challenged the accuracy of its findings. Moreover, although subsequent studies of kibbutz women—including those conducted by scholars affiliated with the kibbutz movement (e.g., Palgi et al. 1983)—were equally critical of its interpretations, nevertheless they confirmed its findings. That being so, it would seem that the anomaly is not apparent, but real. How, then, is it to be explained?

In the light of the arguments raised by the critical reviewers, I would suggest that the explanation lies in the fact that the findings of this study (like those of Tiger and Shepher) constitute a direct, if implicit, challenge to some central assumptions of gender and women's studies, including: (a) gender and gender differences are culturally constructed; (b) the mother's tie to her child is cultural, not natural; (c) female liberation can be achieved just in case the family and child rearing are removed as a focus of women's interests; and (d) the abolition of sex-role differentiation is a necessary condition for sexual equality.

Since these assumptions are regarded as axiomatic, they have never been rigorously tested, not at least in my opinion, and except for some few dissident feminist theorists—for example, Dinnerstein (1976), Elshtain (1974, 1981a, 1981b, 1984), Rossi (1977, 1978, 1984), and Sommers (1992, 1994)—they have seldom been challenged. Although this study admittedly does not constitute such a test—a single case does not have the power to do that—it does, however, constitute such a challenge. For it suggests *pace* these assumptions that (a) gender and gender differences may not be culturally determined; (b) the mother's tie to the child may not be culturally constructed; (c) female liberation may not require that the family and children be displaced as a focus of a woman's interests; and (d) sexual equality may be present, both normatively and actually, even though the social system includes sex-role differentiation.

Seeing that these tentative conclusions were generated by a quasi-experimental longitudinal design, employing naturally occurring events—historical and generational change—as its data base, then by the normative canons of scholarship it might have been expected that rather than ignoring the challenge posed by this study, this challenge would instead have been confronted, either by impugning the evidential relevance of its empirical findings, or by refuting the validity of its theoretical conclusions. Instead, by simply ignoring the existence of this study (and that of Tiger and Shepher), these findings and conclusions alike have been swept under the rug, thereby obviating the need to confront the challenge. In what follows, I wish to briefly summarize the dimensions of this challenge.

## A comparison of the feminist ideology of the kibbutz pioneers and "second wave" feminist ideology

When, in 1951, I began my study of Kiryat Yedidim, a *kibbutz* (communal settlement, pl., *kibbutzim*) in Northern Israel founded in 1921, the kibbutz movement, which originated in the second decade of this century, consisted of 194 kibbutzim, with a total adult population of 67,500. By 1975, the year of my restudy, the figures were 237 and 85,100, respectively, and during my last visit in 1994, they were 270 and 129,300 (Maron 1993:88).

The founders of Kiryat Yedidim, like those of virtually all other kibbutzim founded after World War I, were committed to a feminist ideology that combined elements both of "first wave" feminism (as it has come to be known), which originated some 100 years before the founding of the kibbutz movement, as well as elements of (what is now called) "second wave" feminism, which appeared only in the 1960s, some forty years after its founding. In accordance with first wave (alternatively, "mainstream" or "equity") feminism, one of the goals of these pioneers was the achievement of equity for women, a condition in which they would enjoy the same rights and opportunities (social, economic, political, and educational) as men. But like second wave (alternatively, "gender," or "gynocentric") feminism, these pioneers also had other goals, such as the destruction of "patriarchy" (of which more below) and the abolition of all social differences between the sexes, including (but not restricted to) sex-role differentiation.

The latter goal was critical for the kibbutz pioneers because, like the second wave feminists that were to follow them, they believed that true equality of the sexes cannot be achieved so long as men and women are different, even if their differences are deemed to be of equivalent value (what in this book I call the "equivalence" meaning of equality). Rather, true equality can be achieved, so they believed, if and only if men and women perform the identical social roles and are identical in most other respects as well (what I have termed, in an unfortunate choice of terms, the "identity" meaning of equality).

This conception of sexual equality was motivated by the pioneers' belief that the social and psychological differences between the sexes—in short, their 'gender' differences—are (as contemporary feminists say) "culturally constructed." In other words, they believed that such differences are, on the one hand, a distal consequence of history and tradition, and on the other hand a proximate consequence of childhood socialization.

Although they would not have put it so baldly, the kibbutz pioneers would probably have agreed with those contemporary feminists who argue—as Rossi (1979:715) puts it in her summary of their view—that "the 'only' important sex differences not accounted for by culture are women's ability to menstruate, give birth, and lactate." (See also Elshtain 1981a and Popenoe 1993:7). And since these biological variables, they further argue, have little if any behavioral or psychological relevance, it follows that "if boys and girls are [behaviorally and psychologically] different, they are not born but *made* that way (Thorne 1993:2, italics in original; see also Fausto-Sterling 1985). That being so, it also follows—as Degler puts it in his summary of this view—that "whatever history or socialization had created, human will could undo" (Degler 1990:36).[1]

These views, of course, raise a number of theoretical problems, and much of the early feminist ideology of the kibbutz, like that of contemporary feminism, was designed to cope with them. To mention only two of these problems, if differences in gender and gender-related behavior are culturally constructed, then why is it that they exist in all known human societies? And if, as cultural constructions, these differences can be undone by human will, then why are they so persistent?

Although otherwise sharing the same ideology, it is here that the kibbutz pioneers part company from contemporary feminists, for their diagnoses of these problems and their recommended solutions are very different. For the pioneers, these problems are unwittingly precipitated by the social entailments of the female reproductive system, and hence their solution, so they argued, must be found in the creation of institutional structures that preclude these entailments. For contemporary feminists, however, the problems are created by hegemonic male power, and hence their solution, they argue, consists in the empowerment of females. Let us now examine these different views, beginning with the latter.

For contemporary feminists, differences in gender and gender-related behavior are both universal and persistent because in all societies they serve a patriarchal, political structure by means of which dominant males oppress dependent females. Moreover, in capitalist societies, economically advantaged males oppress economically disadvantaged females, and in multi-ethnic and multi-racial societies, males of superordinate ethnic and racial groups oppress females of subordinate groups (e.g., Glen, Chang, and Forcey 1994). Given this view, it is understandable that whatever the disagreements among them, "each [contemporary] feminist theory or perspective attempts to describe women's oppression, to explain its causes and consequences, and to prescribe strategies for women's liberation" (Tong 1989:1; see also Butler 1990, Lorber 1934, Rich 1980, Shulman 1980, Wallston 1985).

Although contemporary feminists offer various explanations for men's oppression of women, a widespread motivational explanation, frequently more implicit than explicit, is that men hate women. Germaine Greer, for one, does not hesitate, however, to make it explicit. "Male hostility to women," Greer (1992:21) writes, "is a constant; all men hate all women some of the time; some men hate all women all of the time; some men hate some women all of the time."[2]

This motivational explanation for men's oppression of women is arguably carried to its furthest limits by so-called "radical feminists," such as Catharine MacKinnon and Andrea Dworkin, for whom men's hostility to women is most apparent in the aggression that (as they see it) is at the core of male sexuality. Thus, "the male sexual role," MacKinnon (1987:66) writes, "centers on aggressive intrusion on those [i.e., females] with less power," and since "gender inequality is a critical term for the social hierarchy of men over women," it follows that "a theory of sexuality becomes feminist to the extent it treats sexuality as a construct of male power—defined by men, forced on women, and constitutive in the meaning of gender" (ibid.:67). And further:

> Dominance eroticized defines the imperatives of masculinity, submission eroticized defines femininity. So many of the distinctive features of women's status as second class—the restriction and constraint and contortion, the servility and the display, the self-mutilation and requisite presentation of self as a beautiful thing, the enforced passivity, the humiliation—are made into the context of sex for women. This is to identify...sexuality itself as the dynamic of the inequality of the sexes. This is to argue a sexual theory of the distribution of social power by gender, in which this sexuality that *is* sexuality is substantially what makes the gender division be what it is, which is male dominant, wherever it is, which is nearly everywhere. (Ibid.:69)

It should be emphasized that the abstract expression "male dominance" is a euphemism for men's aggression against women at the behavioral level and their hatred of them at the emotional level. Again, MacKinnon writes:

> [Male] force is sex.... Hostility and contempt, or arousal of master to slave; awe and vulnerability, or arousal of slave to master; these are the emotions of this sexuality's excitement.... Violation, conventionally through penetration and intercourse, defines the paradigmatic sexual encounter.... All this suggests that what is called sexuality is the dynamic of control by which male dominance...maintains and defines male supremacy as a political system.... [Pornography] is their [males'] "truth about sex". From its testimony what they want is

women bound, women battered, women tortured, women humiliated, women degraded and defiled, women killed. (Ibid.: 75–76)

This political explanation for the universality and persistence of differences in gender and gender-related behavior is far removed from that offered by the kibbutz pioneers. As the latter saw it, these differences and the sexual inequality they promote are caused instead by the social consequences of the female reproductive system. Briefly put, their argument can be stated as follows: Because it is women who bear children, and because in the traditional family system it is women who rear them, this combination of biological and social variables produces a marriage system in which women, for their own survival and that of their children, are socially and economically dependent on men (their husbands). As a consequence, women's horizons are circumscribed by, and their energies are confined to, the private world of the family, thereby precluding their interest, let alone participation, in the public world of work, politics, science, and art. For the kibbutz pioneers, then, it is these psychological and behavioral consequences of motherhood (in both its biological and social meaning) that are the critical determinants of differences in gender and gender-related behavior.

This theme, it will be recognized, is also prominent in contemporary feminist theory. Consistent, however, with their view that gender differences are culturally constructed, hence an instrument for women's oppression, many (but not all) contemporary feminists regard motherhood as one of the elements of patriarchy. Thus, for Oakley (1974:186) the conception of motherhood is based on the following three beliefs: "all women need to be mothers, all mothers need their children, all children need their mothers." Since, however, these "needs" are cultural, not natural (biological)—the "need" to be a mother, for example, "owes nothing" to the "possession of ovaries and wombs," but is instead a consequence of social and cultural conditioning (ibid.)—motherhood is a "myth" whose purpose is to oppress women. Among other things, this myth "locks women into biological reproduction, and denies them identities and selfhood outside mothering" (Glen 1994:9). (In this connection, see also Firestone 1970, Lorber 1979, and, for a related view, Eyer 1992.)

But if motherhood is culturally constructed, it follows that it can also be deconstructed, and if it is oppressive, then it requires only a small theoretical step to conclude that female liberation requires that motherhood must be rejected. And this is precisely the step that some contemporary feminists, such as Jeffner Allen, have taken. "I would like to affirm the rejection of motherhood," Allen writes (1984:316),

> on the grounds that motherhood is dangerous to women. If woman, in patriarchy, is she who exists as the womb and wife of man.... [a] mother is she whose body is used as a resource to reproduce men and the world of men, understood both as the biological children of patriarchy and as the ideas and goods of patriarchal culture. Motherhood is dangerous to women because it continues the structure within which females must be women and mother and, conversely, because it denies to females the creation of a subjectivity and world that is open and free.

Hence, since motherhood "is men's appropriation of women's bodies as a resource to reproduce patriarchy," (*op. cit.*: 317), then

> [in] the production of the son for the father, in the production of goods for the father, for the benefit of the son, we are not our bodies, we are not ourselves. A means to men's ends, never an end in ourselves, we are selfless, worldless, annihilated. The experience of our servitude takes seriously our danger and holds, firmly and strongly, to the conviction that together we must get out of motherhood. (Ibid: 325)

This, however, is not the theoretical step taken by the kibbutz pioneers. For while they traced sexual inequality to the constraints imposed on women by motherhood, they did not hold that motherhood is a myth, or that the desire for children is culturally constructed, or that biological reproduction is an instrument for the perpetuation of patriarchy. Hence, rather than proposing that motherhood be rejected, these pioneers—consistent with their own views regarding the causes of sexual inequality—proposed instead that marriage (as a legal and economic relationship) and the family (as a residential group) be rejected, and that a radically different marriage and family system take their place. It is their implementation of these proposals, to which we may now turn, that constitutes (what I have called) the pioneers' feminist revolution.

## The pioneers' feminist revolution

To implement their first proposal the pioneers instituted a marriage system in which (as described in the following chapters) each spouse—whether as kibbutz member, as producer, or as consumer—was an independent actor. To implement their second proposal they established a child-rearing system (also described in the following chapters) in which, from birth on, children lived, ate, and slept not with their parents, but in age-graded children's houses, and in which they were reared not by their parents, but by trained caregivers, socializers, and educators.

These revolutionary innovations in child rearing and the family were designed to free the women from the burdens of child care, thereby permitting them to enter those economic and social roles that heretofore had been the exclusive preserve of men, just as the revolutionary innovations in marriage were designed to free them from dependence on their husbands, thereby allowing them to be their equals, both economically and socially. In short, these innovations were designed to promote the equality of the sexes in the sense in which it was understood by the early kibbutz ideology, namely, the "identity" sense of equality.[3]

These innovations—more especially those related to child rearing—were designed, however, not only with the women, but also with the children, in mind. In the latter regard, communal rearing was designed to achieve two educational goals. First, it would preclude the development of emotional problems in children, which, so the pioneers believed, were the inevitable consequence of family living. Second, and much more important for the controversial conclusions of this book, communal rearing, in their view, was the most effective means for transmitting the kibbutz ideology, including its feminist ideology, to the children. Hence, in the children's houses boys and girls were reared in an essentially unisexual regime (Spiro 1958), with the aim that they would internalize the feminist ideology of the kibbutz, and with the expectation that as adults they would exhibit few, if any, gender differences, either behaviorally or psychologically.

This expectation, however, was not fulfilled, and it is this fact, together with its implications for the theoretical understanding of gender and gender differences, that motivated the writing of this book. For when these children—*sabras*, as native-born Israelis are called—became adults, they renounced the feminist ideology of the kibbutz founders; and while they remained and remain committed to the notion of sexual equality in its "equivalence" sense—and what is more they practice it—they have rejected it in its "identity" sense, both in practice and as an ideal.

## The sabras' counterrevolution

If the implementation of the gender ideology of the kibbutz founders constituted a *feminist* revolution, then its rejection by the first generation sabras may be said to constitute a *feminine* counterrevolution, "feminine" on two accounts. First, it was instigated primarily by the female, not the male, sabras. Second, it was motivated both by their wish to return to the sexual dimorphism (ranging from appearance to social roles) that the kibbutz founders had attempted to abolish, as well as by their insistence that the revolutionary institutions created by the kibbutz founders thwarted their needs as females. Hence, in the discussion that follows, the term "sabras," unless otherwise specified, refers exclusively to female sabras.

It need only be added that this counterrevolution is ongoing, for now that the second- (and even third-) generation sabras have come of age, it is evident that they not only have embraced the radical changes initiated by the first generation, they also (as we shall see) have enlarged upon them.

The counterrevolution, it may now be noted, is sweeping in its cope, both ideologically and institutionally. Ideologically, it consists (as I have already mentioned) of the repudiation of the "identity" feminism of the kibbutz founders, according to which women can become the equals of men just in case they become like men (by doing what men do). Indeed, much before Carol Gilligan (1982) and the rise of "difference feminism," the sabras, though feminists, were insisting that there are important and innate differences between the sexes, especially in human relations. Males, the sabras say, are more interested in achievement and dominance, whereas females are more interested in affiliation and nurturance.

These views, as we shall see in later chapters, were expressed by the sabras in Kiryat Yedidim in 1975, and in five other kibbutzim that comprised my (representative) research sample. They were replicated in interviews conducted a few years later in a study of yet another kibbutz conducted by Aviva Zamir (herself a kibbutz member), as the following extracts from her interviews indicate.

*Respondent A*

*Interviewer* : [In referring to sex differences] you seem to be saying that nature is much stronger than our [the founders'] conscious effort to bring about different social conditioning. Your generation seems to reject the idea of equality that we brought you up with.

*Respondent* : The word "equality" is not applicable here. The kibbutz has a problem with the concept of equality. It wants two things: to develop diversity and at the same time to enforce equality.... Do we want equality or do we want resemblance?

*Interviewer* : Meaning what?

*Respondent* : We said we wanted everybody to be of equal value: That is, not equality amounting to resemblance; rather "from each according to his ability, to each according to his needs."...[Hence] one cannot have equal rights in every respect, and at the same time disregard women's rights to acknowledge their own fundamental needs.... [I]f the kibbutz will not give up its main value, namely that each gives according to his ability and each receives according to his needs, then we shall find out what these [the women's] real needs are, the natural needs as well as the ones dictated by society.... It used to be the accepted view that females should be trained to work in agriculture and other male occupations. For me it was always a nightmare.... Why should I work in a branch that does not interest me? I am interested in [working in] education. I like to work with human beings (Zamir 1982:91–93).

*Respondent B*

*Interviewer* : [why are you one of the few women who not only has worked in, but also has been in charge of an agricultural branch?]

*Respondent* : As I said, it is very hard work. And besides, one has to be away from home for long periods of time. That makes it unsuitable for women with children. You cannot ignore the fact that there is a difference between men and women, also true in animals; a difference which is determined by nature.

*Interviewer* : Are you willing to accept it?

*Respondent* : I am willing to accept it.

*Interviewer* : You don't mind personally?

*Respondent* : Of course not. I think that being a woman has many advantages. Giving birth and all that is connected with it is something of which men never experience anything as profound. I have never felt that my sex was inferior, not ever (*op. cit.*:105).

*Respondent C*

*Interviewer* : Do we have equality of sexes in the kibbutz?

*Respondent* : I think there are differences. There are physiological, biological and psychological differences. I am not saying that women cannot be prime ministers or company directors. There are women, not many, who reach the highest positions and fill them successfully. But as a rule women are not equipped to develop the way men do.... It is the woman who bears children and is bound to them more. Even if the husband were to cook and wash and iron, it's still the wife, the mother, that carries the load and creates the bond (*op. cit.*:115).

This ideological counterrevolution of the sabras proceeded in tandem with a counterrevolution on the ground, as is evident from the behavioral and institutional changes they introduced, and which are described in this book. Among others, these include changes in (a) physical appearance, from the founder's renunciation of "feminine" dress and appearance to the sabras' emphasis on these qualities; (b) career preference, from the founders' push for "male" occupations to the sabras' desire for "female" ones; (c) the public arena, from the founders' demand for political and economic leadership positions to their avoidance by the sabras; (d) familism, from the founders' downgrading of the family (including marriage and the domestic household) to the sabras' emphasis on the special importance of marriage and home; (e) child rearing: from the founders' downgrading of the woman's mothering role to its elevation to a position of centrality by the sabras.

As already indicated, these changes had already occurred prior to my restudy of the kibbutz in 1975, but subsequently even more far-reaching changes were introduced, most importantly in mothering and the family. In Kiryat Yedidim (and in the other kibbutzim comprising the federation with which it is affiliated) the latter changes took place only a few years prior to my 1994 trip, but in the other two kibbutz federations they had taken place much earlier. In any event, since these changes took place only after the publication of this book, and since they are arguably the most important index of the sabras' counterrevolution, it is important to describe them here.

As I have already indicated, one (but not the only) purpose for the collective child-rearing system instituted by the kibbutz founders was to implement their feminist ideology and to ensure its transmission to their children. In this system, the children (as I have already noted) lived in age-graded children's houses, though on weekdays they were taken by their parents for a period of two hours after returning from work, and on Saturdays and holidays they took them for a more extended visit. For the kibbutz founders, this child-rearing system, known as "collective education," was the bedrock of kibbutz society. "The kibbutz may undergo many changes, and still remain a kibbutz," I was frequently told in 1950, "but if collective education were to be abolished, that would be the end of the kibbutz [*qua* kibbutz]."

Still, by the middle 1960s some changes in the system of collective education were beginning to appear. Thus, the mothers' workday (but not the fathers') was reduced from eight to seven hours in order to satisfy the mothers' demand to spend more time with their children at the end of the day. But since this change was not sufficient to satisfy this demand—the mothers also wanted to visit their young children during the day—the kibbutzim later instituted (what came to called) the "hour of love," by which mothers with children under one year took a break from their work in midmorning in order to visit with them for half an hour.

Gradually, however, the visiting time was increased to an hour, and it was extended to children of preschool age, as well. Moreover, at about the same time, maternity leave—again at the demand of the women—was extended, and when their leave expired, the mothers' workday was decreased to allow them (rather than the staff of the infants' house) to continue to feed their babies after they were weaned. By the late 1980s mothers did not return to a full work schedule until their babies were 2 1/2 years old.

Despite these changes in collective education, for many sabras they did not go nearly far enough. Collective education, they said, was fine as a day-care system, but as mothers it was their desire, and right, that their children sleep at home. It was "only natural," they maintained, that mothers should want such an arrangement because the present arrangement thwarted their "maternal instincts." In response to these persistent demands, some kibbutzim affiliated with the largest kibbutz federation began to give up "communal sleeping" (*lina meshutefet*) as early as the 1960s in favor of "family sleeping" (*lina mishpachtit*). In short, they began to bring the children home.

Despite this precedent, this far-reaching change in collective education continued to be rejected by Kiryat Yedidim and the other kibbutzim affiliated with its federation, and in 1975, the year of my restudy, communal sleeping was still in place. Indeed, fifteen more years were to elapse before the transition to family sleeping was to occur in any kibbutz affiliated with this federation. The reasons for opposition to family sleeping were multiple.

First, historically the latter federation was always the most strongly committed to the early kibbutz ideology, not only its feminist dimension, but its other dimensions as well. Consequently, even though most first-generation sabra mothers, like some few pioneer mothers, felt frustrated by the system of communal sleeping, still their ideological commitment to this system was strong enough to override their motivation for family sleeping.

Second, for those mothers (and a few fathers) who did not share this commitment, their desire for change was blocked by a simple economic reality—cost. Thus, although by 1975 married couples were living in comfortable two-room apartments, not in the cramped one-room ones they had formerly occupied, even so these apartments were clearly too small to accommodate anywhere from two to five children. (That sabra mothers, on an average, bore twice as many children as their own mothers, is yet another measure of the counterrevolution). Consequently, to bring the children home would have required the construction of new apartments or else the expansion of the old ones. In either case, since the financial outlay for the federation as a whole was estimated in 1984 at $135,000,000 (Bar Lev 1984:35), this cost, even when prorated, was out of the reach of even the wealthiest kibbutzim.

Third, in addition to these ideological and economic constraints, studies of kibbutzim that had adopted family sleeping had demonstrated that this arrangement had important adverse consequences for the mothers. Thus, in these kibbutzim mothers were less active in the cultural and political life of their kibbutz, and participated less in its self-governing institutions than mothers in kibbutzim that had retained communal sleeping (Rosner 1984). Seeing that their evenings (when these activities take place) were taken up with their children, this finding, which strengthened the arguments of the opponents of change, was hardly surprising.

But family sleeping, its opponents pointed out, had still other adverse consequences for the mothers. Thus, whereas in communal sleeping children eat dinner (and their other meals) in the children's house, in family sleeping, however, children come home after school, and the mother must prepare their dinner. In addition, in family sleeping the mother must get up earlier to help dress the children, cook their breakfast, and get them to school. Moreover, with the children at home, it is difficult for mothers to leave the kibbutz on holidays and their days off, much less to take extended leave for graduate studies or refresher courses, constraints that importantly affected their work careers.

Despite, however, these adverse consequences for the mothers, nevertheless this did not diminish their desire to make the change to family sleeping. Although publicly many of them claimed that their desire was motivated by a concern for the children's needs (which made it more acceptable), in fact it was motivated, as Shadmi (1984:58) observed, by a concern for their own (maternal) needs. All available evidence supports this observation.

In the first place, although a few children, as I observed them in 1951, were unhappy with communal sleeping—and as adults they continue to report negative memories of this experience—for the great majority, however, communal sleeping was a very positive experience. To be sure, most of them looked forward to and clearly enjoyed their daily visit with their parents, but based on my observations of them as children and on my interviews with them as adults, it is equally clear that they looked forward to their return to the children's house when the visit ended.

In the second place, interviews with mothers—both of adult and of young children—left little doubt that their desire for family sleeping was motivated not so much by their perceptions of the children's needs, as by their own needs. This is evident not only from interviews I myself conducted in 1975 in Kiryat Yedidim and in five other kibbutzim, and which are summarized in this book, but also from those conducted some years later by other investigators in other kibbutzim.

Among the latter, consider, for example, the following extract from an interview with a mother whose children were already adults:

> For me it is clear that the greatest loss for me as a mother was that I did not have the privilege of raising my children in closer proximity to me, that I did not have the privilege of participating more [in their lives] in the good and in the bad, to cope, to fail and to succeed. That is the true significance of child rearing. We created a beautiful framework, but sometimes it works against the laws of nature. (Rimon 1984:72)

Or consider this extract from an interview with a mother with small children:

> Though [communal sleeping] never caused me any suffering as a child, now, as a mother, I am in favor of ... children sleeping at home. The communal arrangements are quite unnatural it seems to me. There is a conflict here between ideology and emotions.... [A]s a mother, I am dying to have my baby sleep at home, and to see him wake up in the morning. But, ideologically I am apprehensive... because I wish to change the mold of the kibbutz in wanting to switch to family sleeping arrangements.... These are my thoughts, but my feelings welcome the switch. And these feelings are so strong that they have influenced my husband [to vote for the switch, though he opposed it]. (Zamir 1986:41)

Consider, finally, the findings of Ronit Plotnick's quantitative study of 160 kibbutz families, eighty each from five kibbutzim with family sleeping and five with communal sleeping. As reported by Lazar (1994:6), Plotnick, an Israeli developmental psychologist, found that children reared in the system of communal sleeping evidenced no signs of "maternal deprivation," but their mothers suffered from "child deprivation." In short, communal sleeping "created in the mothers a feeling of constant hunger for contact with their baby. This feeling [was] expressed in the need to be more and more with the young infant."

Given this "need" it is hardly surprising that by the early 1990s most of the kibbutzim in the federation with which Kiryat Yedidim is affiliated had made the change from communal to family sleeping. In some, it was instituted by a vote of their members, in others (including Kiryat Yedidim) it was brought about by the unilateral action of the mothers. In any event, today the children of every kibbutz but one are living at home (and from my interviews in 1994, I expect that it too will soon join the ranks).

In short, the second-generation sabra women have done what many (if not most) of their sabras mothers and pioneer grandmothers, *qua* mothers, had wanted to do, but what, *qua* kibbutz members, they were ideologically incapable of doing. I referred above to sabra "women," because while some sabra men favored the change to family sleeping, just as many opposed it, and most, though indifferent, nevertheless agreed to it from a desire to support their wives. One of these men—a first-generation sabra father, and a central player in Kiryat Yedidim—put it this way: "For our parents the kibbutz, not the family, was their focus, and it was the kibbutz to which they dedicated their lives, but they were not happy."

Although not surprised by the comments of this sabra, I (admittedly) was more than a little surprised by those of an old-timer who, when I first met him in 1950, was the chairman of the collective education oversight committee. When, in 1994, I asked him why he had supported the transition to family sleeping, he replied: "Well, it's only 'natural' for a mother to want to have her children with her." My immediate, though silent, interpretation of his change of heart was that it had been brought about under the influence of his daughter, now a mother. But when this man, sixty years a kibbutznick, went on to say, "Isn't it the same among the lower animals?", I was not entirely confident that this was an accurate interpretation.

In any event, while many males supported the transition to family sleeping, it was the females, as I have already said, who insisted upon it; and that they did so, though fully cognizant of the predicted disadvantages that this new arrangement would have for them, is surely a measure of the strength of (as they put it) their "maternal feelings." Moreover, their commitment to this new arrangement remains undiminished even though all these predictions have been born out, not the least of which being inadequate accommodations. Thus, though by 1994, three years following the transition to family sleeping, an extra room had been added to the apartments of families with young children, nevertheless the crowding was (to my eyes at least) oppressive. Yet, despite the crowding, despite the admitted restrictions on their sex lives, and despite the curtailment of their extra-domestic activities, not one woman expressed regret for having made the transition.

## Reply to the critics

I now wish to turn to two of the theoretical issues raised by the counter-revolution: issues related to its possible determinants, on the one hand, and those related to sexual equality, on the other. Although both issues are treated in detail in the body of the book, nevertheless since most reviewers took objection to that treatment, it is perhaps useful to also address them here in the light of those objections. I shall begin with the second, the sexual equality issue.

There can be no doubt that both descriptively and normatively the counterrevolution has been accompanied by the demise of sexual equality in the "identity" sense of equality. To take only two examples, most sabra women, in contrast to the kibbutz founders, value their family and children as much as (and in some cases more than) their careers, and in the latter regard most of them prefer traditionally "feminine" careers over "masculine" ones. It is for these reasons, among others, that the counter-revolution has been uniformly descried by contemporary Israeli feminists (e.g., Agassi 1993, Ben-Rafael 1988:chap. 12, Fogiel-Bijaoui 1992, Palgi 1991, Palgi et al. 1983, Safir 1991, Silver 1991). As they see it, the counterrevolution signals the end of the kibbutz' quest for women's liberation.

This judgment, however, proceeds from their (the critics') conception of sexual equality—the "identity" conception—not the sabras', for most sabra females (as noted previously) have always rejected this conception of sexual equality. If, as they view it, the valorization of a career in the public domain requires the denigration of the private domain of family and children, then this does not signify liberation, but the frustration of their deepest needs as women. But the sabras' rejection of the "identity" meaning of sexual equality does not entail that they have rejected sexual equality, as such, or that they have rejected feminism. Rather they have opted, as we have seen, for the "equivalence" conception of sexual equality—and what is more, they have achieved it—just as they have opted for (what is now called) "difference" feminism.[4]

That these conceptions of "sexual equality" and of "feminism," respectively, signify that women are psychologically different from men in some nontrivial respects, and that these psychological differences entail no small measure of social and behavioral differences, does not bother the sabras. For while they view themselves as different from men, they also regard themselves in every sense as the equals of men. A sabra whom I interviewed in Kiryat Yedidim in 1994 put it this way:

> In my view there are differences in the nature of men and women, and I see no point in denying them. But in the kibbutz this does not mean that men and women are not equal; just the opposite. For here both sexes hold the other in the same esteem.... Although my husband works in production, and I work in services, I have never felt that he had more status just because his work is [economically] profitable and mine isn't.... Of course, I am opposed to discrimination against women, especially when it is forced on us by the religious establishment, and I feel the same about sexual discrimination in the kibbutz. If I believed it existed here, I would fight against it.... But I don't feel it here.... On the contrary, I feel that I am the equal of any male.

These views, not surprisingly, echo those expressed in 1986 by a sabra from another kibbutz who, when asked about job discrimination in her kibbutz, replied:

> In the kibbutz no such problem exists. If a woman were to say that she wanted to study production management, all doors would be open to her.... It is not as if women were trying desperately to achieve certain positions, and were excluded due to their sex. One looks for suitable female candidates, and tries to push them forward towards certain positions, but they don't want to take them on.... In town a man may receive more money than a woman for doing the same job. This, I think, is scandalous. Equal salaries is something worth fighting for. (Zamir 1986:127)

To be sure, there are some who might say that such views reflect these women's "false consciousness," but having observed female sabras over many years, having come to know them both as informants and friends, and having witnessed their relations both with males and females, I myself would reject this hypothesis. On the contrary, I would say that their subjective feelings of being the equals of men, and of being so regarded by men, are realistically grounded.

Let us turn then to the second theoretical issue raised by the counterrevolution, namely, what are its determinants?, or alternatively, how is it to be explained? And in this connection we will also examine the reviewers' near-unanimous misinterpretation of my previous discussion of this issue. In chapter 4, in which I address in particular three aspects of the counterrevolution—mothering, sex-role differentiation, and sexual dimorphism—I construct a typology of their theoretically possible determinants. One type (including various subtypes) consists of determinants "external" to the actors (macrosocial, cultural, and economic); the other (also including subtypes) consists of determinants "internal" to them (motivational). After assessing the evidence for each type, I argue that on balance the counterrevolution is more likely explained by the internal determinants, more especially by desires and needs already present in sabra childhood.

Although I distinguish three types of theoretically possible childhood desires and needs, only one of which is biological, and although I emphasize that from the available data it is not possible to choose among them, nevertheless reviewers, almost without exception, construed my argument as claiming that the counterrevolution had been biologically determined. This misinterpretation is all the more bewildering because latterly biologically oriented social scientists (e.g., Rossi 1984:8–9, Degler 1991:302–303) have pointed to this book as a prime example of the reluctance of social scientists to face up to the importance of biological variables.

How then did the reviewers of the book come to the opposite conclusion? I would hazard two guesses. In the first place, in framing this book I remarked that the study of the counterrevolution in the kibbutz had produced, as it were, a counterrevolution in me. That is, although I had embarked on my kibbutz research in 1950 as a committed cultural determinist, the counterrevolution that I observed in 1975 severely challenged that commitment. For when I became convinced that the counterrevolution had been motivationally determined, and when I came to realize that the motivation consisted of needs and desires which I had observed in female sabras in 1951, when they were young girls—in short, prior to their acquisition of kibbutz culture—the conclusion was inescapable: the needs and desires that motivated the counterrevolution could only have been, so I wrote, "precultural."

Now seeing that cultural (like biological) determinists typically recognize only two explanatory variables, biology or culture, it is possible that the reviewers (mostly cultural determinists) construed my explanation for the counterrevolution as biological because they took the term "precultural" to denote something biological.

My second guess for this misinterpretation, one closely related to the first, is that the reviewers construed the term "precultural" in a phylogenetic sense, not in the ontogenetic sense in which I used it. Briefly, I argued that the motives for the counterrevolution were "precultural" in the sense that they were manifested by sabra girls prior to their acquisition of culture; and although these motives could have been biologically acquired, it was just as likely, so I argued—indeed, I myself believed it to be more likely—that they were socially (i.e., experientially) acquired. If, nevertheless, the reviewers construed the expression "precultural motives" as referring to motives acquired as a phylogenetic inheritance from our precultural ancestors, then that again could explain why they construed my explanation for the counterrevolution as biological.

The irony is that if I were to write this book today, then in the light of what is now known about the evolutionary basis for sex differences, I would indeed argue—together with some contemporary feminist theorists (e.g. Elshstain 1981a, Rossi 1977, 1978, 1984)—that some of the motives for the counterrevolution are precultural not only in the ontogenetic sense, but in the phylogenetic sense as well. I have in mind, for example, the evolutionary differences between the sexes in brains and hormones, and their influence on the observed sex differences in cognition, motivation, and behavior; or the evolutionary significance of the female reproductive system—including menstruation, pregnancy, and lactation—and their influence on females' emotions and behavior.[5]

In sum, considering what is now known about psychological and behavioral significance of only these biological differences between the sexes (e.g., Degler 1990, 1991, Glantz 1989, Hudson and Jacot 1991, Konner 1982: chap. 12, Moir and Jessel 1989, Money and Ehrhardt 1972, Ridley 1993, Stoller 1968), it is hard to escape the conclusion that at least some of the needs and desires that, in my judgment, motivated the feminine counterrevolution, are (as they say) hard-wired. As a prominent feminist sociologist has put it, a gender theory that does not "confront" the biology of sex differences "is an exercise in wishful thinking, and a social science that does not confront it is sterile" (Rossi 1984:15).

It should now be emphasized, however, that the gravamen of reviewers' objections to my explanation for the counterrevolution is not so much that it emphasizes determinants of a biological kind (which in any case is not true), but that it emphasizes *internal* determinants of any kind, biological or not. For in their (cultural determinist) view, the explanation for the counterrevolution is to be found in *external* (more especially cultural) determinants, which some locate in the macrosocial world, others in the microsocial world of the kibbutz. Having discussed both types of external determinants in chapter 4, only however to reject them, I shall not repeat my reasons for doing so here; rather, I shall briefly note some additional reasons.

Those who emphasize macrosocial determinants, namely, the influence on the sabras of the social world outside the kibbutz, fail to recognize that the first-generation sabras, born in the late 1920s and early 1930s, grew up in an era in which, in large degree, the population of Jewish Palestine shared the pioneering values of the kibbutz movement, or else took that movement as their reference group. Admittedly, by 1950 (two years after the creation of the state of Israel), which is when I first encountered them, these sabras (who then ranged in age from 21 to 28) were fully aware that the family, child-rearing, and sex-role systems outside the kibbutz were very different from those found inside, and they were also aware that for most Israelis the kibbutz was no longer their reference group.

Even so, the reviewers who attributed the counterrevolution to the influence of the social world outside the kibbutz failed to address (from their own cultural determinist perspective) two critical questions, the first theoretical, the second factual. In the first place, if, in accordance with their own view, gender identity is formed and gendered activities are determined by childhood socialization and enculturation, then unless the family, child-rearing, and sex-role systems of the outside world held some special attraction for the sabras, why should they have had a more powerful influence on them than those in which they had been socialized and enculturated. And if these systems did in fact have such a powerful influence on them, then, I would argue, it was because they satisfied needs and desires in the sabras that the corresponding kibbutz systems did not satisfy.

In the second place, and perhaps more important, if the influence of the macrosocial world accounts for the counterrevolution, then why is it that this influence was felt primarily, if not exclusively, by the female sabras?

As we have seen, it was the females, not the males, who instigated the counterrevolution, and the males at most only agreed to it. Any credible explanation, surely, must at least be able to account for this basic difference between the sexes.

These two critical questions aside, reviewers who attributed the counterrevolution to the influence of the macrosocial world either ignored or overlooked the critical empirical data that led me to reject that hypothesis. Thus, from the qualitative descriptions and quantitative analyses of children's behavior that my wife and I observed and recorded in Kiryat Yedidim in 1951, it is apparent that long before they had any knowledge of institutions outside the kibbutz, these young children exhibited marked sex differences in their interests and motivations, and what is more the shape of these differences corresponds to the shape of the counterrevolution that they later brought about as adults. Although these childhood data comprise the gravamen of my argument, nevertheless not one of the reviewers who attributed the counterrevolution to macrosocial determinants so much as alludes to these data.

Let us turn now to reviewers who attributed the counterrevolution to determinants in the microsocial world of the kibbutz. Despite the ideological commitment of the early kibbutz movement to sexual equality (in the "identity" sense of equality), there never was a time, these reviewers argue, that any kibbutz had wholeheartedly put this ideology into practice. They point out, for example, that in 1950, when I first arrived in Kiryat Yedidim, this kibbutz (like all others) was characterized by a great deal of sex-role differentiation and, what is more important, the caregivers in the children's houses were all female. As a consequence, the girls, these reviewers argue, must have identified with their female caregivers and, taking them as role models, patterned their behavior on their "feminine" role, and on the "feminine" roles of many other kibbutz women, which in turn accounts for the counterrevolution.

Since this hypothesis is the one that I myself initially adopted, I discuss it in some detail in chapter 4 as well as my grounds for later rejecting it. Here I shall only note some additional grounds. In the first place, even though there was a significant amount of sex-role differentiation in the kibbutz in 1950, nevertheless seeing that the sex differences in the children's behavior resembled the sex differences in adult social roles to only a small degree, it is unlikely that the former differences resulted from adult-role modeling. Moreover, since many of the critical sex differences in the children's behavior paralleled the sex differences reported for children in other and very different societies (Whiting and Edwards 1988), it is much more likely that these differences were (as I subsequently realized) "precultural."

In the second place, if the girls displayed a strong interest in 'mothering' because they identified with the female caregivers, then why, we must ask, did the boys not also identify with them? The conventional answer—that, typically, children identify with adults of their own sex—is convincing only on the hypothesis (with which I agree) that gender is importantly related to sex; for on this hypothesis the boys, by virtue of their male sex, were not motivated to identify with caregivers of the opposite sex. But on the feminist hypothesis of the reviewers that gender has little relation to sex (e.g., Butler 1990, Moore 1994, Ortner and Whitehead 1981, Rosaldo 1980)—the former being cultural, the latter biological—why should the sex of the caregivers have been a disincentive for the boys to identify with them?

Finally, and most important, although in 1950 the children were growing up in a kibbutz many of whose economic roles had become sex linked, nevertheless its revolutionary marriage, family, and child-rearing systems were unchanged, and that was also the case when these children became adults. Hence, even accepting the hypothesis that role modeling explains why it is that the female sabras came to prefer traditionally "feminine" over "masculine" occupations, nevertheless that hypothesis cannot explain why they overthrew the revolutionary marriage, family, and child-rearing systems of the kibbutz, and replaced them with their traditional counterparts.

## Concluding observations

The changes that comprise the counterrevolution described in this book are hardly the only changes that have taken place in the history of the kibbutz movement. On the contrary, the former changes have been accompanied by, and in some cases are related to, many other changes that have occurred over that eighty-year history.

Most of the latter changes occurred in the twenty-five year interval between my first trip to Kiryat Yedidim in 1950, and my second trip in 1975. This was brought home to me when, during the latter trip, a young sabra told me that on a visit he had made to the United States the previous year, he had frequently been asked whether my *Kibbutz: Venture in Utopia*, published in 1955, provided an accurate picture of the kibbutz, but since he himself had not read the book, this query motivated him to do so. His reaction, he said, was "astonishment," for from his perspective the book was a description not of the contemporary kibbutz, the one that he knew, but of its "prehistory."

If this judgment referred to the fundamental structure of the kibbutz or to its quotidian routines, then it was more than a little hyperbolic. If, however, it referred to the ethos and conception of the kibbutz, or to the members' cognitive and motivational orientations, or again to some of their core values, then it was more or less accurate, for by 1975 these had all undergone radical change; and in 1995, twenty years later, they are now entrenched. Let us briefly examine these changes.

1. Change in the ethos and conception of the kibbutz. Under this rubric, the kibbutz may be said to have undergone four interrelated and overlapping changes which, put abstractly and highly schematically, can be characterized as follows:

*From redemptive sect to mundane village.* The founders of the kibbutz, Jewish youth who had migrated to Palestine from Europe, referred to themselves as "the last generation of Exile (*golah*) and the first for Redemption (*ge'ulah*)." Conceiving of redemption as emancipation from the crippling effects of two thousand years of exile, they viewed the kibbutz as the instrument for its achievement. Although this view persisted as late as 1950, by 1975 the kibbutz was viewed not only by the sabras, but also by the founders, as a modern village whose transcendent purpose, even assuming that it still had one, was political, not redemptive.

*From "journey" (derech) to "home" (bayit).* For the founders, the kibbutz was conceived both as a means for the achievement of the twin goals of Zionism and socialism, and also as a template or a model (*degem mofes*) for that "world of tomorrow." By 1975, this conception was all but dead, at least for the sabras, for whom the kibbutz was of value not because it was a means for some higher goal, but because it was home.

*From utopian vision to ordinary social system.* The founders created the kibbutz in order, as they put it, "to discover [the true] man" (*limtzo et ha'adam*). "We have come to the country," as the folk song put it, "to build and to be rebuilt in it" (*livnot u'lehibanot ba*). Already by 1950, however, they had become resigned to the fact that whatever else they had achieved, they had not discovered the new man, nor had the kibbutz created one. For the sabras, who had never entertained such a vision, the kibbutz was but another, if a more humane, social system.

*From fellowship based on love to social group based on rights and duties.* In the early days, the kibbutz was conceived as a fellowship based on bonds of unconditional love, and although formally this conception persisted for many years, by 1950 it was observed more in the breach than in the observance, and by 1975 it was dead even formally. Since then the kibbutz has been conceived more as a corporation than a fellowship, the relationship among its members being based on reciprocal rights and duties, both of which are closely monitored and strongly insisted upon. In short, one might say that the kibbutz has changed from *gemeinschaft* to *gesellschaft*.

2. Associated with the above-mentioned changes in the conception and ethos of the kibbutz are the following changes in the cognitive and motivational orientations of kibbutz members:

*From chiliastic expectations to realistic assessment.* In the early days, kibbutz founders justified their very difficult lives—the poverty, the heat, the malaria, the absence of minimal amenities, the loneliness, the Arab uprisings, and so forth—by the hope of redemption and the anticipation of fulfilling a utopian vision. As these expectations diminished and, beginning already in the 1940s, came to an end, the founders, but more especially the sabras who had never shared these expectations, had to appraise the value and desirability of kibbutz living in terms of more realistic wishes and desires.

*From shared ideology to shared interests as social cement.* No longer united by a strongly cathected transcendent ideal, members increasingly are united not by a common ideology, but by a commonality of interests, including an increase in the standard of living, the enhancement of the quality of life, the welfare of their children, and the like. It is in these terms that today the decision to remain in the kibbutz, or to leave it, is justified.

*From asceticism to consumerism.* Although as late as 1950 the ascetic ideology of socialist Zionism was a central motivational orientation of kibbutz members, that orientation has long been replaced by an emphasis on consumerism. This consumerist orientation is manifest in virtually everything, from the quality of clothing and housing, on the one hand, to the more recent demand for automobiles, on the other. Hence, whereas in the early years, the kibbutz would go into debt only for investment and capital improvement, for many years now it has been willing to incur large indebtedness for improvement in living standards as well.

*From future to present orientation.* For the kibbutz founders, the postponement of present and personal gratification was accepted with resignation, if not equanimity, as necessary for the achievement of more valuable or more important future and collective goals (socialism, the revolution, etc.). With the weakening, if not abandonment of all the grand "isms" (as the sabras put it already in the 1950s), and with the increasing importance of consumerism, the achievement of present and personal gratification has become a cultural imperative.

*From group to private experience.* In the early years of the kibbutz, social interaction and group experience was invested with a therapeutic, if not mystical aura, and privacy was viewed as a form of deviance, if not worse. Hence, evenings were taken up with every kind of group activity, from folk dancing and public confession to intellectual discussion and political debate, which usually took place in the communal dining room, and which went on late into the night. By the 1950s, this group orientation had all but disappeared, and for many years the private apartment has replaced the communal dining room as the center (*merkaz*) for the member's after-work life.

*From "self-realization" to "self-actualization."* As teenagers in Europe, the founders of the kibbutz held that personal growth consisted in each person implementing for himself or herself *(hagshama atzmit)* the goals of socialist Zionism, by migrating to Palestine, settling on a kibbutz, building socialism, and the like. By the 1970s, this notion that the collective welfare (whether that of the nation, the working class, or the kibbutz) was coincident with one's personal welfare had been rejected by the sabras. Instead of "self-realization," they took as their *leitmotif* the very different notion of "self-actualization" *(mimush atzmi),* that is, personal growth through the development of one's talents and abilities whether or not they were useful for the collective welfare.

    3. Change in core values. The changes just described in members' motivational and cognitive orientations have been accompanied by changes

in some few core kibbutz values, of which the following are among the most important:

*Labor: from intrinsic to instrumental value.* For the kibbutz founders manual labor was a paramount value: labor, they said, "is [the essence of] our life" (*Ki ha'avodah hi chayenu*). Their "religion of labor" (*dat ha'avodah*), as it was called, was very much in evidence as late as 1950 (when they were still in their prime), but by 1975 (when the sabras had become the dominant force) it was history. Today, virtually no one desires to perform manual labor, and indeed most such labor is now performed by workers hired from outside the kibbutz, itself a violation of a fundamental principle of the "classic kibbutz" (as it is now called).

*Land: from mystical to pragmatic value.* For the kibbutz founders, it was not manual labor in general, but agricultural labor in particular that was especially valued. They had "gone up" to Palestine in order to work the land, not so much, however, to make a living from the land, as to make a life on the land. Although still regnant in 1950, by 1975 this mystical attachment to the land had been replaced by a pragmatic attitude, according to which agriculture was valuable only to the degree that it was financially sound. Hence, agricultural branches that were no longer profitable (e.g., fruit orchards, olive groves, vineyards, vegetable gardens) were abolished, an attitude that was anathema for many founders. Thus, when a proposal was made in the general assembly of Kiryat Yedidim to abolish the dairy because it was no longer profitable, one of the founders took the floor, exclaiming "Since when did we come here in order to make a profit!"

*Economy: from agriculture to industry.* As agricultural branches have been abolished, they have been replaced by industrial plants of one kind or another, and although the kibbutzim remain the country's largest producers of agricultural commodities, still by the beginning of this decade industry had overtaken and superseded agriculture as the main source of kibbutz revenues (Maron 1993: table 12). This is a far cry from the image of the kibbutz as an agricultural settlement.

*Equality: from radical egalitarianism to qualified stratification.* As a consequence of industrialization, but also of other changes discussed previously, the radical egalitarianism of the classic kibbutz is in danger of becoming obsolete. As late as 1950 all kibbutz labor, skilled or un-skilled, was regarded as equally valuable; each member was viewed as a potential manager of his or her branch; regular rotation in leadership positions, both economic and political, was institutionalized; and all decisions were made by the general assembly, an example (if there ever was one) of direct democracy in pure culture. By the 1970s, however, and increasingly so today, the skilled worker has come to be regarded as more valuable than the unskilled; technical training and superior perfor-mance have become qualifications for managerial positions; central eco-nomic leadership roles have come to rotate only among a highly trained elite; and kibbutz governance is now the function of an elective body, the representative assembly.

An even more extreme departure from the radical egalitarianism of the classic kibbutz is the recent proposal that the present system of equal re-muneration be replaced by a graduated salary scale by which remunera-tion would be calibrated according to a member's efficiency, productivity, and responsibility (*temurah k'neged trumah*). It is still not clear whether this highly contentious proposal will be adopted, but the very fact that it has even been proposed is itself a measure of the challenge to the value of radical egalitarianism.

All the above changes were doubtless influenced by a chain of histori-cal events, both prior to 1975 (the achievement of statehood, mass immi-gration from Near Eastern societies, wars and threats of war, terror and threats of terror) and after 1975 (the ascendancy of the political Right, Camp David, the Intifada, unprecedented economic growth, and national prosperity). Nevertheless, the fundamental influence, I believe, was not these dramatic historical events, but undramatic demographic events, to-gether with their sociological and psychological sequelae, that were oc-curring over that same time period within the kibbutzim themselves.

In brief, in the early years of the kibbutz movement, the typical kibbutz was populated by (a) Eastern European youth in their late teens and early twenties who (b) intent upon creating a new society and a new culture (c) had forsaken their families, homes, and countries of origin, and (d) had "gone up" to live in Palestine. Hence, in its early stage a typical kibbutz, demographically speaking, consisted of a small, single-age, and single-generation cohort whose members, psychologically speaking, were strang-ers in a strange land, and who, sociologically speaking, regarded each other as an undifferentiated, quasi-family group—not, of course, in a biological or a structural sense, but in a psychological, that is, a sentimental and emotional, sense.[6]

However, with the passage of time, the establishment of pair bonds, and the birth of children, this small, single-age and single-generation cohort was transformed, demographically speaking, into a large, multi-age, and multi-generation community, which, sociologically speaking, constituted a differentiated social group consisting of separate biological families and kindred each of whom, psychologically speaking, developed their own centrifugal interests, and so also did their individual members.

It is this chain of events that, in my judgment, were the primary catalysts for the transformation of the classic kibbutz into the kibbutz of today. If, despite these events, the founding generation nonetheless retained to some degree the conception, orientations, and values of the quasi-family kibbutz of their youth, it was because the mystique and élan of that charismatic moment remained with them as an emotionally cathected, nostalgic memory.

This could hardly have been the case, however, for the sabras who had and have no cause to develop nostalgic feelings for a charismatic moment they had never experienced. Moreover, since they did not acquire and, in the nature of the case, could not have acquired any functionally equivalent emotional incentives for perpetuating a sociocultural system that in large measure was the creation of the historical, sociological, and psychological variables that produced that charismatic moment, the changes they have made in that system are not only understandable, but also, so I would argue, predictable. Since, however, this book is only concerned with the changes that constitute the feminine counterrevolution in the kibbutz—ideological changes in the conceptions of women, gender, and gender equality, and structural changes in the institutions of marriage, family, and child rearing—that argument is perhaps best deferred for another occasion.

## Notes

1. The view that gender differences are culturally constructed implies, of course, that gender and gender differences came into being only after the origin of culture, and although this is very far from my understanding of primate social behavior (or of mammalian social behavior more generally), this implication is explicitly insisted upon by at least some contemporary feminist anthropologists. Thus, Zihlman (1993:49), a biological anthropologist, writes:

   I do not believe the term "gender" applies to non-human primates, and I therefore reserve its use for human behavior and its implicit symbolic base and social construction. [Even]...for early hominids of 2 to 4 million years ago which are still very much like apes, I also use "sex" rather than "gender."

Again, in the first chapter of a collection of essays on the cultural construction of gender and sexuality, the author postulates the existence of a nongender stage in human cultural evolution, and moreover describes its social and cultural concomitants (Cucchiara 1981:chap. 1). To which I would join Glantz (1989:92) in asking: "What creature is he [Cucchiara] talking about? An Australopithecine? *Homo erectus*? The Neanderthals?"

Although the editors of this collection, in their otherwise exemplary introduction, admit that Cucchiara's discussion is "essentially a thought experiment," nevertheless they placed it, they say, at the beginning of the volume because it conveys "the sense in which gender is a cultural (and social and historical) construct," and hence it has the purpose of "unhinging the reader's mind from standard modes of thinking about gender-related matters" (Ortner and Whitehead 1981:6; see also Lorber 1994:6).

2. Although Greer goes on to say that "unfortunately, women cannot bring themselves to hate men," this view is not shared by all contemporary feminists. Thus, the feminist literary critic Jane Tompkins (1993:37) writes: "anger is what fuels my engagement with feminist issues; an absolute fury that has never even been tapped, relatively speaking. It's time to talk about this now, because it's so central, at least for me. I hate men for the way they treat women, and pretending that women aren't there is one of the ways I hate most."

3. It is probably no accident, sociologically speaking, that the abolition of marriage and the family, at least in their traditional forms, was also an important part of the agenda of many of the utopian communities that sprang up in the United States in the last century (e.g., Kolmerten 1990, Lauer and Lauer 1983, Muncy 1973, Wagner 1986, Wayland-Smith 1981).

4. This sets the kibbutz apart from the nineteenth-century American utopian communities that aspired to equality in the identity sense, but achieved it in neither sense, as the references cited in footnote 3 indicate.

5. As I have already noted, some contemporary feminists trivialize the emotional and behavioral significance of menstruation, pregnancy, birth, and lactation by claiming that they comprise the "only" biological differences between the sexes. Other feminist writers go even further by arguing that some of these ostensible biological events are in fact cultural. Thus, according to Rapp (1993:123), "reproduction is increasingly understood as cultural not natural."

6. The emotional texture of these early family-like kibbutzim is evidenced in personal documents—letters, diaries, reminiscences, testimonies, and the like—many of which, fortunately, are preserved in kibbutz archives. Non-Hebrew readers may find a small sample of these documents in Near's magisterial history of the kibbutz movement (Near 1992: esp. pp. 40–41, 81, 246).

Because I arrived in Kiryat Yedidim some thirty years after its founding, the family-like stage in its development was only a memory, so that I was unable to witness it firsthand. Still, by tapping into the memories of some of its founders—then in their forties and fifties—I was able to glean at least some appreciation for the emotional texture of this stage (Spiro 1955:53–55). Since then, however, the personal documents from this period were collected and published in a collection (Shadmi et al. 1988) that comprises a treasure trove for students not only of the early days of Kiryat Yedidim, but of the kibbutz movement more generally. Equally important is the volume by Nathan Shaham (1984), himself a member of Kiryat Yedidim, which unfortunately has not been translated into English.

# References cited

Agassi, Judith Buber
    1993    "Theories of Gender Equality: Lessons from the Israeli Kibbutz."
            In Yael Azmon and Dafna N. Izraeli (eds.), *Women in Israel:
            Studies of Israeli Society, Vol. VI*. New Brunswick, N.J.: Trans-
            action Publishers.

Allen, Jeffner
    1984    "Motherhood: The Annihilation of Women." In Joyce Trebilcot
            (ed.), *Mothering: Essays in Feminist Theory*. Totowa, N.J.:
            Rowman and Allanheld.
Bar-Lev, Shlomo
    1984    "Hata'aleh Hamishpacha L'shilton B'kibbutz?" *Hachinuh
            Hameshutaf* 112: 35–42.
Ben-Rafael, Eliezer
    1988    *Status, Power, and Conflict in the Kibbutz*. Avebury: Addershot.
Cucchiara, Salvatore
    1981    "The Gender Revolution and the Transition from Bisexual Horde
            to Patrilocal Band." In Sherry Ortner and Harriet Whitehead (eds.),
            *Sexual Meanings: The Cultural Construction of Gender and Sexu-
            ality*. Cambridge: Cambridge University Press.
Degler, Carl N.
    1990    "Darwinians Confront Gender." In Deborah L. Rhode (ed.), *Theo-
            retical Perspectives on Sexual Differences*. New Haven: Yale Uni-
            versity Press.
    1991    *In Search of Human Nature: The Decline and Revival of Dar-
            winism in American Social Thought*. New York: Oxford Univer-
            sity Press.
Dinnerstein, Dorothy
    1976    *The Mermaid and the Minotaur*. New York: Harper and Row.
Elshtain, Jean Bethke
    1974    "Moral Women and Immoral Man." *Politics and Society* 4: 453–73.
    1981a   "Against Androgeny." *Telos* 47: 5–22.
    1981b   *Public Man, Private Woman: Women in Social and Political
            Thought*. Princeton: Princeton University Press.
    1984    "Symmetry and Soporifics: A Critique of Feminist Accounts of
            Gender Development." In Barry Richards (ed.), *Capitalism and
            Infancy*. London: Free Association Books.
Eyer, Diane E.
    1992    *Mother-Infant Bonding: A Scientific Fiction*. New Haven: Yale
            University Press.
Fausto-Sterling, Anne
    1985    *Myths of Gender: Biological Theories about Women and Men*.
            New York: Basic Books.
Firestone, Shulamith
    1970    *The Dialectic of Sex*. New York: Bantam Books.
Fogiel-Bijaoui, Sylvie
    1992    "From Revolution to Motherhood: The Case of Women in the
            Kibbutz." In Deborah S. Bernstein (ed.), *Pioneers and Home-
            makers: Jewish Women in Pre-State Israel*. Albany: State Uni-
            versity of New York.
Gilligan, Carol
    1982    *In a Different Voice: Psychological Theory and Women's
            Development*.Cambridge: Harvard University Press.

Glantz, Kalman
    1989    *Exiles from Eden: Psychotherapy from an Evolutionary Perspective*. New York: Norton.
Glen, Evelyn Nakano, Grace Chang, and Linda Rennie Forcey (eds)
    1994    *Mothering: Ideology, Experience, and Agency*. New York: Routledge.
Glen, Evelyn Nakano
    1994    "Social Constructions of Mothering: A Thematic Overview." In Evelyn Nakano Glen, Grace Chang, and Linda Rennie Forcey (eds), *Mothering:Ideology, Experience, and Agency*. New York: Routledge.
Greer, Germaine
    1992    "The Backlash Myth." *The New Republic* 207: 20–22.
Hudson, Liam, and Bernadine Jacot
    1991    *The Way Men Think: Intellect, Intimacy and the Erotic Imagination*. New Haven: Yale University Press.
Kolmerten, Carol A.
    1990    *Women in Utopia: The Ideology of Gender in the American Owenite Communities*. Bloomington: Indiana University Press.
Konner, Melvin
    1982    *The Tangled Wing: Biological Constraints on the Human Spirit*. New York: Holt, Rinehart and Winston.
Lauer, Jeanette, and Robert H. Lauer
    1983    "Sex Roles in Nineteenth Century American Communal Societies." *Communal Societies* 3: 16–28.
Lazar, Yaacov
    1994    "Anah Pantah Ha'ahavah." *Hadaf Hayarok* (28 June 1994).
Lorber, Judith
    1979    "Comment." In Harriet Engel Gross et al. *Considering "A Biosocial Perspective on Parenting."* *Signs* 3: 695–717.
    1994    *Paradoxes of Gender*. New Haven: Yale University Press.
MacKinnon, Catharine A.
    1987    "'A Feminist/Political Approach: Pleasure Under Patriarchy." In James H. Geer and William T. O'Donohue (eds.), *Theories of Human Sexuality*. New York: Plenum Press.
Maron, Stanley
    1993    *Kibbutz in a Market Society*. Ramat Efal: Yad Tabenkin.
Moir, Anne and David Jessel
    1989    *Brain Sex: The Real Difference Between Men and Women*. London: Michael Joseph.
Money, John and Anke A. Ehrhardt
    1972    *Man and Woman Boy and Girl: The Differentiation and Dimorphism of Gender Identity from Conception to Maturity*. Baltimore: Johns Hopkins University Press.
Moore, Henrietta
    1994    "Gendered Persons: Dialogues Between Anthropology and Psychoanalysis." In Suzette Heald and Ariane Deluz (eds), *Anthro-*

*pology and Psychoanalysis: An Encounter Through Culture.*
London: Routledge.

Muncy, Raymond Lee
1973    *Sex and Marriage in Utopian Communities: Nineteenth Century America.* Bloomington: Indiana University Press.

Near, Henry
1992    *The Kibbutz Movement: A History. Volume I, Origins and Growth, 1909–1939.* Oxford: Oxford University Press.

Oakley, Ann
1974    *Woman's Work: The Housewife, Past and Present.* New York: Pantheon Books.

Palgi, Michal
1991    "Motherhood in the Kibbutz." In Barbara Swirski and Marily P. Safir (eds.), *Calling the Equality Bluff: Women in Israel.* New York: Pergamon Press.

Palgi, Michal, Joseph Raphael Blasi, Menachem Rosner, and Marilyn Safir (eds).
1983    *Sexual Equality: The Israeli Kibbutz Tests the Theories.* Norwood, Penn.:Norwood Editions.

Popenoe,David
1993    "Parental Androgogeny." *Society* 30: 5–11.

Rapp, Rayna
1993    "Reproduction and Gender Hierarchy: Amniocentesis in America." In Barbara Diane Miller (ed.), *Sex and Gender Hierarchies.* Cambridge: Cambridge University Press.

Ridley, Matt
1993    *The Red Queen: Sex and the Evolution of Human Nature.* New York: Macmillan.

Rimon, Lurit
1984    "Symposium Bichtav Likrat Moetzet HKBH"A." *Hachinuh Hameshutaf* 112: 71–72.

Rosaldo, M. Z.
1980    "The Use and Abuse of Anthropology: Reflections on Feminism and Cross-cultural Understanding." *Signs* 5: 389–417.

Rosner, Menahem
1984    "V'adayin hareshut Netuna." *Hachinuh Hameshutaf* 112: 21–26.

Rossi, Alice S.
1977    "The Biosocial Basis for Parenting." *Daedalus* 106: 1–31.
1978    "The Biosocial Side of Parenting." *Human Nature* 1: 72–79.
1979    "Reply by Alice Rossi." In Harriet Engel Gross et al. *Considering "A Biosocial Perspective on Parenting."* *Signs* 3: 695–717.
1984    "Gender and Parenthood." *American Sociological Review* 49: 1–19.

Safir, Marilyn P.
1991    "Was the Kibbutz an Experiment in Social and Sex Equality?" In Barbara Swirski and Marily P. Safir (eds.), *Calling the Equality Bluff: Women in Israel.* New York: Pergamon Press.

Shadmi, Menachem
    1984    "Nesiga Oh Shinui, Vikuach Al Goralo Shel Hakamuna."
            *Hachinuh Hameshutaf* 112: 54–59.
Shadmi, Eli, Zvi Tsameret, Muki Tsur, and Ruth Beit-Or
    1988    *Kehilyatenu: Hegot, Levatim, V'ma'avei Chalutzim.* Jerusalem:
            Yad Yitzhak Ben-Zvi.
Shaham, Nathan
    1984    *Ha'har V'habayit.* Tel Aviv: Sifriat Poalim.
Silver, Vivian
    1991    "Male and Female Created He Them." In Barbara Swirski and
            Marily P. Safir (eds.), *Calling the Equality Bluff: Women in Is-
            rael.* New York: Pergamon Press.
Sommers, Christina Hoff
    1992    "Sister Soldiers." *The New Republic* 207: 29–33.
    1994    *Who Stole Feminism? How Women Have Betrayed Women.* New
            York: Simon and Schuster.
Spiro, Melford E.
    1955    *Kibbutz: Venture in Utopia.* Cambridge: Harvard University Press.
    1958    *Children of the Kibbutz.* Cambridge: Harvard University Press.
Stoller, Robert J.
    1968    *Sex and Gender: On the Development of Femininity and Mascu-
            linity.* New York: Science House.
Thorne, Barrie
    1993    *Gender Play: Girls and Boys in School.* New Brunswick: Rutgers
            University Press.
Tiger, Lionel, and Joseph Shepher
    1975    *Women in the Kibbutz.* New York: Harcourt-Brace-Jovanovich.
Tomkins, Jane
    1993    "Formative Strategies." In Diane P. Freedman, Olivia Frey, and
            Frances Murphy Zauhar (eds.), *The Intimate Critique: Autobio-
            graphical Literary Criticism.* Durham: Duke University Press.
Tong, Rosemarie
    1989    *Feminist Thought: A Comprehensive Introduction.* Boulder:
            Westview Press.
Wagner, Jon
    1986    "Sexuality and Gender Roles in Utopian Communities: A Criti-
            cal Survey of Scholarly Work." *Communal Societies* 6: 172–88.
Walston, Barbara Strudler
    1985    "Feminist Research Methodology from a Psychological Perspec-
            tive: Science as the Marriage of Agentic and Communal." In
            Marilyn Safir, Martha T. Mednick, Dafne Israeli, and Jessie Ber-
            nard (eds.), *Women's Worlds: From the New Scholarship.* New
            York: Praeger.
Wayland-Smith, Ellen
    1981    "The Status and Self-Perception of Women in the Oneida Com-
            munity." *Communal Societies* 8: 18–53.

Whiting, Beatrice Blyth, and Caroline Pope Williams
  1988   *Children of Different Worlds: The Formation of Social Behavior.*
          Cambridge: Harvard University Press.
Zamir, Aviva
  1986   *Mothers and Daughters: Interviews With Kibbutz Women.*
          Norwood, Penn.: Norwood Editions.
Zihlman, Adrienne L.
  1993   "Sex Differences and Gender Hierarchies Among Primates." In
          Barbara Diane Miller (ed.), *Sex and Gender Hierarchies.* Cam-
          bridge: Cambridge University Press.

# Foreword

Melford Spiro is a recognized authority on the Israeli kibbutz—a social experiment that is, moreover, an ongoing way of life. Spiro's book *Kibbutz: Venture in Utopia* (1955) established this authority; his second book on *The Children of the Kibbutz* (1958) went beyond this and secured for him the position of one of the most distinguished psychological anthropologists in this country. The present volume, third in the series, is highly relevant to the modern theme of women's rights. It is safe to say that henceforth no argument, either pro or con, will be complete without the findings of this engrossing book being taken into account.

The nature and the accurate discrimination of male / female differences within their common humanity have probably preoccupied people since the beginning of at least human time. Two sharply contrastive views have emerged. One, most conspicuously exemplified by Margaret Mead, might be termed the *ethnological*, i.e., that masculine / feminine psychological differences are based on inculcated expectancies that differ culturally and are learned. Thus, on one single though large island in Melanesia, Mead found the Arapesh, among whom both sexes were nurturant-"feminine" in occidental terms; the Mundugumor, with both sexes aggressive-"masculine"; and the Tchambuli, in neat paradigm, with females "masculine" and males "feminine."[1]

The contrasting view is that masculine / feminine "tertiary" sexuality (primary = genital, secondary = hormonal, tertiary = psychological, temperamental) is *ethological*, i.e., based in some manner on given panhuman anatomical differences. Possibly the ethnological explanation of Mead is still currently regnant because of its availability for the arguments of the women's liberation movement. It is also consistent with a Boasian tradition that emphasized, for earlier

1. Margaret Mead, *Sex and Temperament in Three Primitive Societies* (New York: W. Morrow & Co., 1935.

and honorable antiracist purposes, the purely cultural differences *sui generis* of Ruth Benedict's relativism, with no possible biological-racist basis.

In the last twenty years, however, there has emerged a holistic psychobiological anthropology that goes beyond mere ethnographic description, and attempts to reach dynamic and biologistic explanations of the observed phenomena. In the holistic view,[2] with which Spiro correctly identifies the present writer, human sexual dimorphism—anatomical, hormonal, and temperamental alike—is seen to be fundamental in the very formative "hominization" of the species. A few words are needed to present this more complex modern view.

In contrast with the merely foraging and only occasionally meat-eating ecology of larger primates such as anthropoids and baboons, the first "human" revolution—the active hunting of animals for meat with weapons by all-male groups—was critical to the species-specific nature of human nature, including human sexual dimorphism. Thus, anatomically, human males are generally larger than females, with more massive musculature and bones, and relatively fat-nude for the purpose of radiating body heat produced through the expenditure of massive amounts of energy as in hunting.[3] Longer-legged males are adapted to a more rapid metabolism physiologically also, in their larger lungs and larger number of oxygen-carrying red blood cells per cubic centimeter. But shorter-legged females do not need to be adapted

2. Weston La Barre, *The Human Animal* (Chicago: University of Chicago Press, 1954); a more complete treatment, which takes into account major advances in the new primatology, may be found in *The Ghost Dance* (New York: Delta Books, 1972), pp. 73–89 on hominization and pp. 100–107 on sex typing. See also "Personality from a Psychoanalytic Viewpoint," pp. 65–87 in Edward Norbeck, Douglass Price-Williams, and William M. McCord (eds.), *The Study of Personality: An Interdisciplinary Appraisal* (New York: Holt, Rinehardt & Winston, 1968), and "Anthropological Perspectives on Sexuality," pp. 38–53 in Donald Grummon and Andrew M. Barclay (eds.), *Sexuality: A Search for Perspective* (New York: Van Nostrand Reinhold Co., 1971).

3. Loss of slower-foraging primates' body-hair in humans is a further step, in the presumably tropical-African habitat of early hominids. Caucasoid males are hairier than Negroid perhaps because they reached higher latitudes (where insulating body hair would be adaptive) before this process was complete, whereas for Negroids remaining longer in the same tropical habitat the process continued. So, too, the specialization in increased darkness of skin in some Africans (black, from a generic primate and mammalian brown) still further facilitates the diffusion of body heat, as indeed would also the marked linearity of males in some African groups. (Any residual "male-bonding" and instinctual "aggressiveness" in modern males from the hunting experience of early hominids I regard as unproven in fact and dubious in theory, inasmuch as hunting with weapons is *cultural*, and cultures notoriously change.)

like wild animals to hunting, for they are domesticates (protection from natural wild enemies, man-provided food, and selective breeding are the technical criteria for domestication). That is, the human female is removed by the male from the wild-animal state of self-provision. At the same time, male meat-sharing from a common enterprise in group hunting, provides a higher-protein commodity for selective favoritism in sharing with females, whence the beginning of marriage regulations and emergence of the kin-family within the social-primate band. Shorter-legged females, with more subcutaneous fat and less rapid metabolism, can then specialize in reproduction and child care. For group survival under primitive conditions, childbearing may have been of necessity almost continuous: the temporary mammalian breast becomes permanent in the human female, just as the menstrual cycle replaces seasonal oestrus and is concomitant with nonseasonal year-round breeding, and sexuality-motivated family cohesion. If marriage is strongly female-motivated economically, then exclusiveness of sexual claim would appear to be male-motivated for obvious reproductive-economic reasons, judged also from the commonness and economic base of polygyny and the comparative rarity of polyandry.

In a (more correctly) "trimorphism" in the nuclear family, the human infant, as big-brained at birth as a widened female pelvis can permit, can in turn specialize in mother-nurtured infancy, with still-continued brain growth in a "premature" (noninstinct-prepared) learning animal, whose whole postcranial growth is largely postnatal. Moreover, as we know from the fossil series, brain size progresses phylogenetically as well in hominids, as if brains were an adaptive trait. But dependence of infantile individuals is meanwhile a biological burden on adults, hence prolonged infancy must have some adaptive advantage for the group. This advantage, so the argument goes, is culture, which enables individuals and societies to tap the larger past experience of the whole species, as if culture (and language) in this big-brained social species were more adaptive than fixed instincts.

In the holistic view, which takes into account both human biology and culture, *specialized* maleness and femaleness *and* infancy in the familial trinity are all intrinsic to the species' humanity. That the startling and problem-laden reproductive *success* of this species and the adaptive potential of human symbiotic culture have resulted in cultural "speciations" far removed from early hunting and gathering ecologies, does not impugn the functional importance of adaptations during the period of hominization, but rather confirms them. Nor have all traces of this formative specialization yet disappeared biologically under these newer conditions. Thus, holistic anthropology is consistent with Freud's observation that, psychosexually, "anatomy is destiny."

The Israeli kibbutz has been an authentic social experiment, as this important book will demonstrate. The utopian feminism of early earnest socialism sought the emancipation of women through basic changes in the traditional system of marriage, the family, and sex-role differentiation. Nevertheless, as Zwi Shatz observed, "the need for the family is very deep and organic." For it was women, not men, who progressively brought children back from the common nursery-dormitory to the nuclear family home. And by their own choice, women gradually withdrew from heavy agricultural work (despite the greater ideological prestige of "productive" jobs) in which they were intrinsically "not interested," whereas men by similar free choice regravitated from the "service" to the heavier agricultural jobs.

Thus, whereas the pioneer kibbutzim had had a cultural explanation for sex-role differentiation, the kibbutz-reared sabra would argue a biological one. There is no note of macho crowing at what has transpired in the quarter century between Spiro's two fieldtrips. Both sexes appear to be content with what has happened. Spiro himself hesitates to ascribe the dramatic reversion of early idealistic, utopian, radical feminism either to an "inevitable" return to discernible "basic" human nature, or a counterrevolutionary return, oedipal revolt abreacted and spent, to a markedly patriarchal Jewish cultural tradition. Instead, Spiro's careful, judicial reporting and controlled methods explore every alternative logical explanation. It is Spiro's notable openmindedness and painstaking logic that increase our confidence in his conclusions. The "new human beings" turn out to be very human indeed. In the words of one founder of the Kiryat Yedidim kibbutz, "We came here to discover man." Perhaps they did—in all this species' complex ambiguity.

Perhaps also there are elements of a third alternative view of why females appear to have some chronic dissatisfaction with the feminine role, for males do have real psychic burdens in a masculine role as well. But males are able to understand females only in the projective terms of their own anatomy[4]—and both sexes have mutual anxieties attendant upon these differences—hence males may have a chronically distorted view of female sexuality, and females are bound obscurely to resent this male misunderstanding, under no matter what cultural dispensation. And even as a learning experience, living in a female body is bound to be different from the experience of living in a male body, so that even ontogenetically "tertiary" masculinity and femininity have this inevitable biological base. If so, then it is still true in this special sense that, psychosexually, "anatomy is destiny."

Biological time during man's hominization has been far longer than any subsequent cultural-speciation period. Yet, to maintain a rigorously biological view, it remains equally obvious that, in the drastically altered new demographic and ecological predicaments of contemporary *Homo sapiens*—just as the earth's environing conditions (e.g., of early absence and later presence of atmospheric oxygen) have changed during the evolution of life itself—so, too, the biosocial conditions to which humanity must now adapt may offer as yet unexplored evolutionary predicaments and adaptive opportunities both for women and for men. Nevertheless, with respect to biological givens in contemporary *Homo sapiens*, Spiro's data repeatedly and consistently demonstrate that in Israeli kibbutzim the "feminist revolution" has been reversed in a "feminine counterrevolution" and that, in shaping sex roles, "precultural" (psychobiological) forces are still prepotent over cultural (sociopsychological) ideologies.

Weston La Barre

---

4. No moral fault of either sex is the evolutionary accident that, in all endoskeletal animals, there has been a three-hundred-and-fifty-million-year battle between the genital and the urinary functions for an opening to the outside world (for phylogenetic details, see *The Human Animal*, 2nd edition, 1968, pp. 340–41). A confusion of orifices, and of menstruation with castration, as well as of genital / excretory substances, may also contribute to the notion that sexuality is dirty and dangerous, in a male view of female sexuality.

# Preface

It might be assumed that the question of the relative influences of nature and culture on human affairs had long been laid to rest. Nevertheless, this little book—an expansion of the Jensen Lecture delivered at Duke University in 1976—is concerned with that very question. Although substantively devoted to the changing roles of kibbutz women, the latter question raises theoretical issues that transcend the kibbutz; namely, to what extent are differences in male and female orientations to marriage, family, and work culturally determined, and to what degree can these orientations be changed by social engineering? To raise these issues is not to suggest that kibbutz women are not important in their own right, but only to say that the implications of the kibbutz situation should command the serious attention not only of kibbutz specialists, but of every student of female psychology, on the one hand, and of the cultural dimensions of human nature, on the other.

Actually, this book is an intellectual spin-off from an inquiry that in its inception was concerned neither with women nor with sex roles —indeed, I had not even read the burgeoning literature dealing with the current interest in these subjects until I had completed the first draft of my manuscript—but with culture, and more particularly with the relationship between culture and human nature. The roots of this inquiry go back to 1951, when, accepting as axiomatic the widely held social science view that human beings have no nature— or, to put it differently, that human nature is culturally constituted and, therefore, culturally relative—I embarked together with Audrey Spiro on a study of child rearing and personality development in the kibbutz I call Kiryat Yedidim. This kibbutz being thirty years old at that time, my aim was to discover the dimensions of the revolution in human nature which, ex hypothesi, had been brought about by the social and cultural revolution effected by the kibbutz movement. (For a description of these children and of the kibbutz revolution see Spiro, 1958 and 1955, respectively.) In 1975 I returned to Kiryat

Yedidim in order to follow the course of what was perhaps the most important (because voluntary) sociocultural revolution in our century.

Although in the intervening quarter century, many changes had occurred in the kibbutz, it was clear that, with one exception, the foundations of its revolutionary social and economic structure had become firmly grounded. The exception consisted of the relationship between the sexes—in the domains of marriage, the family, and sex-role differentiation. In these intervening twenty-five years, dramatic changes had occurred in these institutions, which, however, were in the direction not of their revolutionary, but of their prerevolutionary (traditional), forms. Hence, although I was not primarily interested in sex roles, these changes inevitably engaged my attention because they, at least, seemed to challenge the axiom—the cultural relativity of human nature—which had been the point of departure for my original study of kibbutz children. In short, although I had conceived of the present study as one of social change, I found myself confronted once again with the nature-culture problem.

As a study in social change, my research proceeded from a model which is rather different from what seems to be the dominant model for such studies. The latter model assumes that the history of a social group is the history, as it were, of a perduring corporate entity, so that social change, like individual change, is viewed as occurring in the same entity that had previously been characterized by the status quo ante. Sometimes, as when a particular generation changes an institution which it itself had practiced, this model (although surely false) presents no obstacle to understanding. This is not the case, however, when the innovators comprise a different generation from the one that practiced the prechange institution. In the latter case, the appropriate question is not why the group—taken as a perduring corporate entity—has changed its institution at this particular time in its history, but why this particular generation has changed an institution practiced (if not instituted) by its predecessors.

The very nature of the case examined here forces the second model upon us. The adults studied in Kiryat Yedidim in 1975 were the children we had studied in 1951, and the counterrevolutionary changes that they have brought about in the relationship between the sexes constitute a departure from the revolutionary institutions which had been created by the previous kibbutz generations, rather than from those that they themselves had practiced. This being so, the question which must be addressed is not why the kibbutz, viewed as a corporate group, has undergone important changes in its orientation to marriage, family, and sex-role differentiation, but why the present kibbutz generation has instituted such changes. Moreover, since this generation had been raised in and inculcated with the revolutionary orientations of the kibbutz founders, to explicitly address the latter question is to implicitly address another: do these changes represent the triumph of the old culture over the new, or do they represent the triumph of nature over culture? These are the questions with which this volume is ultimately concerned.

Although most of the material presented here describes the contrast between the situation found in Kiryat Yedidim in 1951 and that found in 1975, the dramatic changes that have taken place in that kibbutz are especially important inasmuch as they have been duplicated to a greater or lesser degree in the entire kibbutz movement. This generalization is based on various sets of data; first, studies of individual kibbutzim by other investigators; second, the statistical summaries dealing with the kibbutz movement as a whole compiled by Tiger and Shepher (1975) in their impressive, and the first, full-length study dealing with this topic; third, a survey of the internal publications of individual kibbutzim, as well as of the various kibbutz federations; fourth, my own study of a sample of six kibbutzim. I should briefly describe the latter study.

Although I had little reason to doubt that the findings of my 1975 study of Kiryat Yedidim were representative—most especially because they were corroborated by the large-scale study of Tiger and Shepher which had been published that very year—I was nevertheless concerned to assess my interpretations of these findings. Hence, in 1976 I returned to Israel in order to survey a sample of *sabras* (those born and raised in the kibbutz) in six other veteran kibbutzim, two from each of the three major kibbutz federations. In each kibbutz, ten adults (five males and five females) born and raised in the kibbutz—making a total sample of sixty subjects—were chosen for intensive interviews dealing with all facets of kibbutz life including, but not restricted to, marriage, family, and sex-role differentiation. Although this survey, together with the time entailed in analyzing and coding the interviews, delayed the final preparation of the manuscript for two years, the delay was minor relative to the

importance of checking the findings and interpretations of the Kiryat
Yedidim study. The results were unambiguous: the interview data
from these kibbutzim provided strong support for the conclusions derived from my participation-observation study of Kiryat Yedidim.
Nevertheless, since the longitudinal data are derived exclusively
from the latter kibbutz, the ethnographic descriptions found in this
volume are primarily based on observations made in Kiryat Yididim.

This volume, and the research on which it rests, was made possible
by many persons and institutions. First, I wish to express my appreciation to the lectureship committee for the invitation to deliver the
Jensen Lecture. To Weston La Barre, my gracious host at Duke, I
am indebted for encouraging me to expand the lecture to book length,
and for consenting to write the Foreword. To Leslie Y. Rabkin, I am
indebted for generously making available the data he collected in
his follow-up study of Kiryat Yedidim in 1966–68. (See the last chapters in the second editions of Spiro 1955, 1958.) As a consequence
I was able to return to Kiryat Yedidim in 1975 with a great deal of
knowledge concerning the changes that had transpired in the intervening quarter century. I am especially indebted to my wife, Audrey
Spiro, who in 1951 conducted a study of early childhood behavior in
Kiryat Yedidim. Without her invaluable data, which comprise part
of the larger discussion of child behavior in chapter 4, I would not
have been able to properly interpret what I observed in 1975.

To Menachem Rosner and Menachem Gerson, whose efforts made
it possible to conduct the sample surveys in 1976, I am most grateful.
In the latter connection, I am especially grateful to Hagar Tchizik,
who conducted these interviews with skill and tact while I interviewed
the kibbutz leaderships. We are both grateful to the six anonymous
kibbutzim that offered us their generous cooperation and hospitality.
Above all, however, I am grateful to my friends and comrades of
Kiryat Yedidim who in 1975, no less than in 1951, permitted me to
participate in their lives.

Research requires funds and writing demands leisure. A research
grant from The National Institute of Mental Health supported my
research in Israel in 1975 and 1976, and a Guggenheim fellowship,
together with a sabbatical leave from the University of California,
provided the freedom from normal academic responsibilities that
enabled me to write this book. I am deeply thankful to all three.

I wish to thank Sheri Komen and Janet Loomis for their patience in typing and retyping the many abortive drafts that finally became a manuscript. The following individuals read and criticized all or parts of the manuscript: Rae Blumberg, Menachem Gerson, Sheila Lesniak, George Saunders, Shirley Strum, and Marc J. Swartz. Although I did not always follow their advice, I want to thank them for their assistance.

# Gender and culture

To admit that the fulfillment of some of our ideals may in principle make the fulfillment of others impossible is to say that the notion of total human fulfillment is a formal contradiction. . . . For every rationalist metaphysician . . . this abandonment of the notion of a final harmony, in which . . . all contradictions are reconciled, is . . . an intolerable bankruptcy of reason. . . . The world that we encounter in ordinary experience is one in which we are faced with choices between ends equally ultimate, the realization of some of which must involve the sacrifice of others . . . [If men] had assurance that in some perfect state, realizable by men on earth, no ends pursued by them would ever be in conflict, the necessity and agony of choice would disappear, and with it the central importance of the freedom to choose. Any method of bringing this final state nearer would then seem fully justified. . . . If, as I believe, the ends of men are many, and not all of them are in principle compatible with each other, then the possibility of conflict—and of tragedy—can never be wholly eliminated from human life. . . .

Isaiah Berlin, *Two Concepts of Liberty*

# Chapter 1. The ideology of female liberation

## Introduction

Although seldom included in any set of basic human characteristics, the imaginative projection of ideal states of existence is nevertheless, I would submit, one of the unique characteristics of our
species. Whether expressed in the private fantasies (day dreams and
night dreams) of ordinary individuals, articulated in the sophisticated
creations of philosophers and novelists, or represented in the myths
and eschatologies of social groups, these imaginative projections indicate—or so it seems to me—that most individuals and groups, finding their immediate reality wanting, have a need to construct an
imaginary state of affairs—an ideal reality—in which the perceived
deficiencies of the immediate reality are temporarily overcome, if not
permanently transcended. Now that primate research is discovering
protosymbols, protolanguage, and prototool traditions—in short, pro-
toculture—among many species of infrahuman primates, perhaps
protoprojected ideal states of existence will also be discovered among
our primate cousins. At the moment, however, it seems safe to assume that the symbolic capacity (if not the emotional need) to construct an imaginary reality which represents an improvement of
many orders of magnitude over an actual reality is a species-specific
characteristic of *Homo sapiens*, in short, a distinctive attribute of
human nature.

When this ideal state of affairs is projected as a group rather
than merely an individual goal, when it is conceived as attainable by
human rather than divine action, and when it is believed that its actualization can occur in the natural order rather than in some other
order, such as heaven or paradise, such an ideal reality is designated
as a *utopia*. Most utopias share three rather interesting, though unrelated characteristics. First, the utopian vision (as distinguished
from other visions of an ideal reality) seems to be peculiar to Western culture. Why this is so is a fascinating question, but one not ger-

mane to our topic. Second, although many individuals and groups have had utopian visions, few attempts have been made to actualize them, and—if I may be permitted another sweeping generalization—these attempts have occurred only since the industrial revolution. Third—and this may tell us as much about human nature as about the need to project ideal states of reality—the vast majority of actualized utopias are short-lived, coming to an end if not during the lifetime of their founders, then shortly thereafter. It is because the kibbutz movement—the utopian movement in Israel—is an exception to this latter generalization that it is (among other reasons) of particular interest for any theory of human nature and its social and cultural vicissitudes.

Founded in 1910, the kibbutz movement has already been witness to its grandchildren growing into adulthood as members, workers, and leaders of their respective kibbutzim. Moreover, although it has had to abandon its self-image as the vanguard of and the model for the next stage in social evolution, the kibbutz movement has been successful not only by virtue of its survival, but by any other criterion by which the success of social systems is evaluated. Growing from one kibbutz with a few score members, to 240 kibbutzim with 100,000 members, this movement has proven to be highly creative in a variety of social, economic, and cultural domains. Comprising only 3 percent of the total Israeli population, the kibbutzim produce 33 percent of the gross national farm product, 5 percent of the gross national industrial product, and 12 percent of the total gross national product. During the last decade for which information is available (1957–1967), their average annual economic growth was 2.5 percent, the average annual growth of their property value per economic unit was 11 percent, and the average annual increase in their net income was 3.8 percent. (French and Golomb 1970:21). Again, the kibbutzim provide a disproportionately large percentage of the officers of the Israeli army, members of parliament, and cabinet ministers. One-third of the cabinet of the last government, for example, were kibbutz members. Finally, the kibbutzim have by all odds the best schools in the country, a disproportionately high percentage of the country's novelists, poets, painters, and sculptors, and—on a different note—a disproportionately low percentage of its criminals. One murder and one embezzlement comprise the total recorded crime committed by kibbutz members in the history of the kibbutz movement.

The utopian vision of the founders of the kibbutz movement comprised no less than the creation (as they put it) of a "new man." Viewing human beings as essentially good, but as having been corrupted by bourgeois culture and urban civilization, they believed that it was only necessary to strip them of their bourgeois and urban excrescences for their true nature to emerge. In the words of one of the founders of Kiryat Yedidim, "We came here to discover man," that is (he went on to explain), to uncover that love and kindness, that sense of fellowship, that altruistic concern for others which the kibbutz pioneers believed to comprise man's basic nature. To uncover these qualities, they wanted to create a social system in which science ("reason") rather than religion ("superstition") was to inform its world view; in which cooperation, based on the sentiment of brotherhood, was to be the dominant mode of social relations; in which goods and services were to be produced and distributed according to the guiding principle of "from each according to his ability to each according to his needs"; in which radical egalitarianism, both social and economic, was to be practiced; in which everyone was to be a worker (and hired labor repudiated); in which the means of production (including land), as well as all other capital goods (including housing), were to be publicly owned; in which pure democracy was to be practiced, and to be institutionalized in a manner which would preclude anyone from acquiring power over anyone else; in which children were to be freed from the domination of parents and raised with a maximum of freedom in a community of peers; and—to come to the topic of this book—in which women were to be fully emancipated. The last aim was to be achieved by a radical transformation in the traditional systems of marriage, the family, and sex-role differentiation.

## The ideology

Some three generations prior to the rise of the contemporary women's movement, the founders of the kibbutz movement proclaimed as one of their historical missions the total emancipation of women from the "shackles"—sexual, social, economic, and intellectual—imposed on them by traditional society. In 1950, some forty years after the founding of the first kibbutz, an important kibbutz journal proudly claimed that the goal of sexual equality had been achieved.

We have given her [the woman] equal rights; we have emancipated her from the economic yoke [of domestic service]; we have emancipated her from the burden of rearing children; we have emancipated her from dependency on the husband, her provider and commander; we have given her a new society; we have broken the shackles that chained her hands.

In order to evaluate these claims, it is necessary to examine the explanation offered by early kibbutz ideology for sexual inequality in traditional society, as well as its conception of the meaning of "sexual equality."

Kibbutz ideology, formulated jointly by males and females, rejected the two most frequently offered explanations for the existence of sexual inequality. On the one hand, it rejected the usual innate explanations—those that assume the genetic inferiority of women, as well as those that attribute the social differentiation of men and women to their biological differentiation. On the other hand, although hardly blind to the advantages reaped by males from the traditional system of sexual inequality, it also rejected a currently prevalent social explanation that represents this system as a conscious or unconscious attempt by men to exploit women. Rather, kibbutz ideology took a somewhat different tack, attributing sexual inequality to what it termed "the biological tragedy of women."

This rather dramatic expression refers to the social and cultural restraints imposed on women by virtue of their mammalian reproductive system. Since females bear children, and since as mothers they have the major responsibility for caring for them, they are tied to what kibbutz ideology termed "the yoke of domestic service," while men are free to work in extradomestic domains. This system of sex-role differentiation was held to be the core of sexual inequality, and from this core all of its other facets were believed to follow. First, since men work in the higher status, extradomestic occupations, while women are restricted to low status domestic work, women are inferior to men in the social domain. Second, restricted to nonincome-producing work, the wife is economically dependent upon her husband, so that women are subordinate to men in the domestic domain. As still another consequence of her economic dependence upon him, the wife's social status is merged with that of her husband's, so that the woman's identity as a social person is submerged in his. Third, because domestic responsibilities consume all their time and energy, women have neither leisure nor motivation to pursue positions of political leadership. Hence, they are subject to the authority of men in the political domain. Finally, and for the same reasons, women rarely have the opportunity to express their intellectual and artistic talents and are therefore inferior to men in the cultural domain.

Although the female reproductive system, according to this analysis, is the cornerstone of the entire edifice of sexual inequality, kibbutz ideology rejected the notion that anatomy (to employ a currently fashionable metaphor) is destiny. For although it is a biological imperative that women bear children, it is not a social imperative that mothers care for them. Hence, if a social system were created in which mothers were relieved of the burden of child rearing, the chain of social consequences set in motion by women's reproductive biology, so it was believed, would be reversed. Its first effect would be the dissolution of the sexual division of labor—hence, the attainment of sexual equality—in the economic domain, which, in turn, would assure sexual equality in the domestic, political, and cultural domains. The abolition of economic sex-role differentiation—both the hallmark of, and the means to, full sexual equality—required in the first instance radical changes in two core institutions of traditional society, marriage and the family, and this is precisely what the kibbutz movement proceeded to do. Before describing these changes, however, it is important to explicate with greater precision the conception of sexual equality espoused by the kibbutz ideology.

Equality, it is obvious upon slight reflection, has at least two meanings, both in popular as well as in technical usage. According to one view, people are said to be equal if, but only if, they are similar if not identical with respect to one or more criterial attributes. This might be characterized as the "identity" meaning of equality. According to a second view, people are said to be equal (even if they are dissimilar with respect to the criterial attributes) so long as their differences are held to be of equivalent value. This view, which might be characterized as the "equivalence" meaning of equality, is based on a pluralistic system of values, one in which the different forms assumed by the criterial attributes are viewed as having (more or less) the same worth. Applying these two meanings of equality to the problem of sexual equality, then, according to its "identity" meaning, men and women are not equal if, with respect to the attribute of occupation, for example, they are dissimilar. According to the "equivalence" meaning, however, the sexes may be said to be equal so long as their differences with respect to this attribute are held to be equally valuable.[1]

It is clear, from our capsule description, that the ideology of the early kibbutz movement (like certain aspects of the ideology of the contemporary women's movement) subscribed to the "identity" meaning of sexual equality. Viewing the domestic activities that are related to women's reproductive biology, and that are traditionally conceived as "feminine"—child bearing, child rearing, homemaking, and the like—as inferior to and of lesser value than those extradomestic activities that are traditionally viewed as "masculine," this ideology held that women could achieve equality with men if, but only if (economically at least), they became like men.[2] Indeed, for the pioneer women any kind of sexual differentiation—including sexual dimorphism—was viewed as a symbol of female inferiority, and hence to be minimized as far as possible. Consequently, the artificial enhancement of this dimorphism was viewed as a demeaning substitution of sexual attractiveness for personal achievement as the means for attaining status and power. For this reason, the women discarded dresses and skirts in favor of the baggy trousers and shorts worn by men, and they disdained the use of other traditional means of enhancing feminine charm. Cosmetics, beauty care, perfume, jewelry, and feminine hair styles were all rejected as stigmas of an

1. After completing the first draft of my manuscript, I discovered that Rossi, although not using these terms, had already enunciated this distinction between these two meanings of sexual equality in a balanced and elegantly reasoned paper (Rossi 1977). I discovered, too, that this distinction is also implicit in a recent paper by Sacks (1976). Without using these terms, Sacks argues that sexual equality in its "equivalence" meaning is possible only in noncapitalist societies, whereas its "identity" meaning (which she calls the "state bias") is the form required by the capitalist state. Although I do not find this argument persuasive, my criticisms need not be spelled out here, especially since some of them are implicit in the following discussion.

2. That is why the expression, "the biological tragedy of women," was not intended as a cliché, but as a deeply felt conviction. The very expression, of course, reflects an extremely negative view of those values traditionally conceived as "feminine," and (as in the case of the contemporary women's movement) the women held this view even more vigorously than the men. Consciously, of course, it is not the female but her traditional role that is viewed as inferior if not demeaning by such attitudes. It is at least open to conjecture, however, that these attitudes might also reflect an unconscious demeaning attitude toward the female herself, or, at least, toward female biology.

inferior status. To be the equals of men, women were to become like men not only in their occupational roles, but in their external appearance as well. It was as if the women felt that to achieve equality with men, they had to reject their femininity.

Whatever the personal motives for the women's view of sexual differentiation as tantamount to sexual inequality, the historical and ideological roots of this view are clear. The founders of the kibbutz movement, most of them emigrants from eastern Europe, were greatly influenced by the Russian Revolution on the one hand, and the European youth movement on the other. The "ideal heroine" of the progressive young Jewish women of Poland and Russia, as Tsur (1975:51) has observed, was

> the young Russian woman revolutionary who severed relations with her middle-class home and values in order to dedicate herself to changing society and woman's condition. The Jewish daughter no longer identified herself with her mother the homemaker, but with the woman who chose prison, was exiled, or was condemned to death in her struggle as a nurse in the villages, helping the peasants, preparing herself and others for the new world which would be born in the victory of the Revolution.

Some of these Jewish women attempted to actualize these new images as revolutionaries in eastern Europe; others—those who helped found the kibbutz movement—as *chalutzot*, pioneers of the Jewish national liberation movement in Palestine.

But their decision to become Zionist pioneers had important consequences for the women's notions of sexual equality. Since the kibbutz was (and to a great extent remains) a farming community, its important, economically required occupations were agricultural, and since it was also a socialist-Zionist community, these occupations were simultaneously those that were culturally prized. That the founders of the kibbutz movement, urbanites all, should have instigated one of the few reversals of an evolutionary sequence—from rural to urban settlement and from farm to industrial production—is a paradox that demands a brief explanation since it has important implications for our subsequent analysis.

According to socialist-Zionist ideology, the national liberation of the Jews required not only their return to their ancient homeland, but the wholesale transformation of their historically conditioned diaspora mentality. This transformation, moreover, entailed a return to farming, for by tilling the soil they would (a) learn once again to identify with nature, (b) become physically productive, and (c) discard the superficial and corrupting culture of urban life. Hence, although the founders of the kibbutz movement had emigrated from a society in which physical labor was symbolic of low status, physical (and especially farm) labor became for them the mark of the highest status. Conversely, business, commerce, the liberal professions, and the like, were disdained as self-seeking (if not exploitative) "careerism."

Since, then, farm labor represented the cynosure of Zionist-socialist ideology, and since the pioneer women of the kibbutz movement subscribed to the "identity" meaning of sexual equality, whose core was economic equality, they—no less than the men—insisted on performing strenuous farm labor. That, traditionally, the latter was a male specialty did not deter them because, as good cultural determinists, they were convinced that sex-role differentiation (like any other dimension of the social system) is culturally determined, and therefore historically alterable. This is not to say, however, that the pioneer men supported them in their resolve. Although the formal ideology of the kibbutz movement was unequivocally feminist, this ideology was formulated by a second generation of kibbutz pioneers who had been trained in various socialist-Zionist youth movements prior to their emigration from Europe. Within the first generation—those who had migrated to Palestine prior to World War I—women encountered strong opposition from the men when they attempted to enter agricultural and other types of physical labor that had formerly been male monopolies. It was only through strong determination and firm resolve (see Shazar, 1975, and Maimon, 1962) that this first generation of pioneer women was able to overcome the resistance of their male comrades. Hence, when the later pioneers, including those who founded Kiryat Yedidim, founded their respective kibbutzim, the women's feminist aspirations were not only articulated in a well-formulated ideology, but the groundwork for their implementation had already been laid by the efforts of their predecessors.

## Institutional implementation

To attain its goal of sexual equality, it was necessary, according to kibbutz ideology, to radically change the institutions of marriage and the family. It should at least be noted, however, that the attainment of this goal was not the only motive for these institutional changes. Thus, the changes introduced in the family were intended to achieve at least two other goals. First, they were viewed as a means for the liberation of children from the "patriarchal authority" of the father. Second, based on the premise that the welfare of the group is an ultimate value (and that competition and concern for private ends are inimical to this value) and on the belief that group participation is a consummatory goal (and the pursuit of privacy is a moral defect), changes in the family were also instituted in order to create a new human being, one for whom these values are internalized as essential characteristics of human nature. So far as the latter goal is concerned, the sentiments of love, affection, and cooperation, which traditionally were associated with the family, were to be transferred from the family to the collectivity; that is, the kibbutz itself was to become a "family." Zvi Shatz, a founder of the kibbutz movement, put it this way:

> The family of the past, or the kvutzah [kibbutz] of our future life—that is the real and permanent refuge that will save the soul of man. . . . In the life of the kvutzah may be found the special atmosphere within which the characteristics of the new man can be formed. . . . The family is being destroyed. . . . But the eternal life values will remain and only their form will change, because the need for family environment is very deep and organic. . . . On the basis of spiritual, not blood ties, the family will be reborn—and in the form of small, modest work groups. (Quoted by Emi Hurwitz, in Neubauer 1965: 355–56.)

This could be achieved, so it was assumed, if the children were raised in peer groups, rather than in family groups. Hence a system of "collective socialization" was to replace the system of family socialization.

In addition to the achievement of female emancipation, changes in marriage were also motivated by the ideological emphasis on the primacy of the collective, for the exclusiveness that character- izes the marriage bond was viewed as inimical to this all-important value. Hence, although marriage was not to be abolished, its im- portance was to be minimized, for kibbutz ideologists seemed to have agreed with Max Weber in viewing the exclusiveness formed by sex- ual bonding as a threat to group identification. This is how Smetter- ling, one of the founders of the kibbutz movement, put it: "As compared with love in general, the love of two people for each other is a matter of the most private choice. That is what separates couples from the rest of the members, and encloses them as an 'isle of the happy' against whose shores beat the waves of collective living" (quoted by Emi Hurwitz, in Neubauer 1965:356).

Insofar as changes in marriage and the family were motivated by the desire to achieve sexual equality, they were instituted to free the women from the "yoke of domestic service." To achieve this end it was believed necessary in the first place to relieve the mother of the responsibility of caring for her children. This was to be ac- complished by the system of "collective socialization" (*chinuch meshutaf*), in which children are assigned from birth to age-graded children's houses, where the responsibility for their socialization is delegated to child care specialists. Although children visit their par- ents daily, and parents in turn visit the children, the latter play, study, eat, and sleep in the children's houses. In effect, this means that although the kibbutz family—parents and children—exists as a social group, it is not (at least it was not) a residential group.

But the dissolution of the family as a residential unit was viewed not only as an important sociological, but as a crucial psychological, step for the achievement of sexual equality. For unless her children were dislodged from a position of affective centrality in her life, the conflict engendered in the mother by her emotional attachment to her children, on the one hand, and her aspiration for self-realization through extradomestic labor, on the other, would constitute a serious obstacle to the ultimate breakdown of sex-role differentiation—the hallmark (according to kibbutz ideology) of sexual equality.[3] By

3. The inner conflict experienced by the early female pioneers in Palestine who were committed to their work as well as to their family was described by one of the participants in the following way: "And this internal inner division, this double pull, this alternating feeling of unfulfilled duty—today toward her

means of collective socialization, moreover, mothers (and, of course, fathers, too) would come to view children less particularistically (as "my children") and more universalistically (as "kibbutz children"). As the cultural symbol of this normative perception of children and the mark of the desirable redistribution of the woman's emotional attachments, I would instance a practice of the very early days of the kibbutz. All mothers nursed their babies in the infants' house in the same room and at the same time, after which the babies were weighed, not only to make sure that they had received sufficient nourishment, but that they had received equal nourishment. If it was then ascertained that some babies had received more milk than others, their mothers were expected to put them aside in order to offer their breasts to those babies whose mothers had provided them with less milk. This practice, long discarded, was consistent not only with the early kibbutz notion of radical social equality, but with the belief that if female emancipation was to be achieved, the particularistic mother-child bond must be displaced from the focus of the woman's emotional attachments.

But for women to be fully emancipated from domestic duties, it was not sufficient that they achieve freedom from child care. It was necessary, as well, to create still another set of communal institutions —a communal kitchen, a communal dining room, a communal laundry, and so on—whose intent was to relieve women of all housekeeping responsibilities. No longer confined to the domestic domain, women would be free to take up extradomestic occupations. These institutions achieved not only their intended economic effect, but also their intended effect on the character of the marriage relationship. For in becoming self-supporting, the wife had become independent of her husband not only economically, but socially as well. Since her labor, no less than his, contributed directly to the collective (rather than merely the domestic) welfare, her social status derived from her own talents and accomplishments, rather than being a reflection of her husband's. In short, the wife had become a social person in her own right. To further emphasize her separate identity, the wife (in the early years of the kibbutz) not only retained her maiden name, but she maintained her separate status as a kibbutz member independently of her husband's membership. The individ-

---

family, the next day toward her work—this is the burden of the working mother" (G.M., in Shazar 1975:211).

ual spouse, rather than the conjugal pair, was the social unit of the kibbutz.

To dilute the cultural meaning of marriage, mates were characterized merely as a "couple" (*zug*), and spouses designated each other either as "comrade" (*chaver*), or as "young man" (*bachur*) and "young woman (*bachura*), never as "husband" (*ba'al,* literally "master") and wife (*isha*). To further undermine the traditional conception of the conjugal bond and the notion of the wife as subordinate to the husband, the traditional marriage ceremony was rejected, and instead marriage was legitimized in the kibbutz by granting the couple a joint room. Moreover, almost as if to deny their relationship (and consistent with the kibbutz fear of the anticollective exclusiveness of the conjugal bond), spouses almost never showed affection for each other in public, they avoided sitting together in the kibbutz dining room or in other public places, and (since housing was in short supply) they frequently shared a room with a bachelor. In short, whatever psychological meaning their marriage might have had for the conjugal pair, structurally it merely entailed their co-residence.

With this we have completed our sketch both of the kibbutz ideology concerning sexual equality and the institutional changes that were introduced for its implementation. If these cultural and structural variables are, as it were, the input variables of the system, we must now examine its output variables, i.e., we must describe the system as it looks, as they say, on the ground. In doing so, we must attend especially to sex-role differentiation, marriage, and the family.

# Chapter 2. The vicissitudes of institutional change

## Sexual division of labor

Although in the early history of the kibbutz movement, men and women, in accordance with kibbutz ideology, worked in the fields side by side, it became apparent fairly soon that the attempt to abolish sex-role differentiation in the economy did not entirely achieve the expected results. First, their ideology of cultural determinism notwithstanding, the pioneers soon discovered that (so far as work at least is concerned) biology *is* a variable: most women came to realize that they were incapable of performing certain agricultural jobs —field crops, for example—as adequately as most men. Simply put, they lacked the requisite stamina and strength. In addition, the relatively high incidence of miscarriages in the early history of the kibbutz was attributed by doctors to the fact that women worked with heavy equipment, such as tractors; hence, women who wanted to bring their pregnancies to term were disinclined to continue such work. As a result, many transferred from the more strenuous agricultural to the less strenuous horticultural branches, such as the vegetable gardens, vineyards, and fruit orchards.

But this was only one basis for the development of a sexual division of labor. It is obvious that some division of labor, whether based on sex or some other criterion, is necessary in any society; even in a farming community, some members must perform non-farm labor. Hence, although most women were freed from their traditional "feminine" tasks (cooking, laundering, sewing, and the like) by the transfer of these activities to communal institutions, it was decided for still other biological reasons to be noted below that these "service branches" (as the kibbutz designates them) should become female specialties. As a result, as farm workers women were not only concentrated in horticultural rather than agricultural occupations, but many were withdrawn entirely from work on the land.

As the kibbutz changed from a childless community to one with children the process of sex-role differentiation became intensified. Although the abolition of the family as a residential unit relieved mothers of the responsibility for child care, it was necessary that they be replaced by specialists in the communal rearing of children. Again, it was decided (at least partly for biological reasons) that these occupations—nursing, nursery teaching, school teaching—should become female specialties. Moreover, since babies were (and are) breast-fed, mothers of young babies withdrew temporarily or permanently from work on the land to work in service branches because the latter were in closer proximity to the infants' house.

Since the decision that many service branches, as well as child care, should become female specialties was made jointly by males and females, the reemergence of sexual specialization in the kibbutzim can hardly be represented as the reemergence of male chauvinism; that in some cases, however, it represented the reemergence of sex-role typing (on the part of both sexes) can hardly be doubted. Often, however, it was based on a hard-boiled economic calculus. Being poor, sometimes desperately poor,[1] the early kibbutzim required high productivity for both consumption and investment goals, and since in general, male farm labor was more productive than that of females —both because of the men's stronger physique and because their labor was not interrupted by pregnancy and nursing—the transfer of many women to service branches was based as much on economic consideration as on sex-role typing.

In any event, by 1950, the very year that the kibbutz movement was proclaiming that its goal of female emancipation had been achieved, and thirty years after the founding of Kiryat Yedidim, a sexual division of labor, following fairly traditional lines, had become a fact of life in all established kibbutzim. In Kiryat Yedidim, for example, only 12 percent of the able-bodied women were working

1. The following statement, by a female founder of one of the earliest kibbutzim, gives some flavor of the conditions under which they lived: "Our poverty oppresses the individual, makes it impossible for him to satisfy his personal needs in accordance with his own appetite and taste. The heavy work, the constant tiredness, the blazing heat, the poor food, the life in tents and barracks, the impossibility of taking one decent rest in the course of the year, to refresh oneself with the sight of the world—these are the real causes of our dark moods and our bitterness" (Lelia Bosevitch, in Shazar 1975: 149).

on the land, while 88 percent worked in services, child care, and education. Moreover, in the quarter century that has passed since 1950, the sexual division of labor has become accentuated, for although its basic structure has not changed, the percentage of women in the farming branches of the kibbutz economy has declined even further. There are at least four reasons for this decline. First, the horticultural crops in which women had been represented in 1950, have generally been replaced by new agricultural crops, such as cotton, both because they are capital, rather than labor intensive, and because they are more profitable. Second, the kibbutz birth rate has escalated, demanding even larger numbers of women in child care activities. Third, some service branches, such as secondary education, which in 1950 had been staffed primarily by males, have become predominantly female. Finally, sabra females (born and raised in the kibbutz) do not share their mothers' and grandmothers' motivation to work on the land. Since this last reason touches on one of the major concerns of this book, I shall discuss it later in detail.

For all these reasons, even in Kibbutz Artzi, the most radical of the four kibbutz federations and the one most concerned with women's liberation, only 9 percent of the women are currently engaged in some type of farming activity; and even if they are combined with those who work in industry—contrary to its original ideology, most kibbutzim are now heavily involved in industrial production—it is still the case that only 12 percent of the female labor force is permanently assigned to productive branches, compared to 50 percent in 1920. (Anonymous 1969:13). More illuminating, perhaps, is the sexual distribution of the labor force in the several branches of the economy. In this same federation, males comprise 87 percent of the farm workers, 77 percent of the industrial workers, and 99 percent of the construction workers. Conversely, females comprise 84 percent of the service workers and the educational workers (Tiger and Shepher 1975:90–91).

As a partial balance to this picture, however, it must also be noted that there has been at least a trickle of males into certain service branches which, in the past, had been exclusively female. Thus, for example, in 1975 the general manager of the communal kitchen in Kiryat Yedidim, as well as the dietician, were males; and although the head cook was female, that position too had been held by a male —a major, incidentally, in the army reserve—the year before. This would have been unheard of even as late as ten years ago. Similarly, males now relieve the regular female personnel in the children's houses, albeit on Saturdays only, and strictly on a rotation basis. It might also be observed, from the other side, that although in the past the principal of the high school in Kiryat Yedidim had always been a man, today that post is held by a woman.

The marked sex-role differentiation in the kibbutz economy, and especially the near-absence of women in farm work, is not at all what the pioneer women had originally envisioned or hoped for. Subscribing as they did to the "identity" meaning of sexual equality, a meaning which signifies the absence of sexual specialization, it is little wonder that even prior to 1950 the "problem of the woman" (ba-ayat ha-bachura) had become one of the pressing problems of the kibbutz movement. (As we shall see below, this was not, however, the only basis for the "problem.") More interesting, however, than this predictable reaction of the pioneer women in 1950 is the perhaps unpredictable stance of the sabra women in 1975. If the latter—the daughters and granddaughters of the pioneers—are only infrequently found in the farming branches, it is not because these branches have become de facto male specialties, but because the great majority have no desire to enter them. For the sabra women farm labor is neither intrinsically fulfilling, nor a necessary symbol of sexual equality. Simply put, the need of the pioneer women to demonstrate their equality with men by successful achievement in physically demanding farm labor is no longer an issue among contemporary kibbutz women. They do not subscribe to the "identity" meaning of sexual equality.

Sabra women not only reject this meaning, but many of them also reject the premise of the feminist ideology of the kibbutz founders from which it is derived—the premise that sex-role differentiation is culturally determined. They feel that this differentiation is biologically determined. This view, as the following extract from an interview with a young sabra woman in 1950 indicates, was also found twenty-five years ago. What was then, however, an indiosyncratic belief has become today the received opinion. "I think that a woman should do the work for which she is suited; not on tractors or in the fields. Women, by nature, cannot be active in agricultural production, particularly if their family life is to be integrated. Of course, some do it, and they do it in Russia. Still, I think it's not natural." In short, by 1975 it had become the view of most sabra women—and of sabra men as well—that the kibbutz division of labor, in which men work in farming and women in nonfarming labor, is a result of innate sexual differences. Women, they say, are most fulfilled by working with and helping other people, while men are most fulfilled when working with machinery and in tasks which give them a sense of power and domination.

This change in attitude toward sex-role differentiation, and its institutionalization in a system of sexual specialization, is symbolized by (and even further institutionalized in) a radical innovation in the curriculum of kibbutz high schools. Whereas, in 1950, any sexual differentiation in education was opposed by the kibbutz movement, today, in addition to the academic courses which remain coeducational, manual arts courses are offered for the male students, domestic science for the female.

The changing views of kibbutz women concerning economic specialization do not imply, I hasten to add, that they are entirely content with the economic roles available to them in the present division of labor. But their discontent (the sources of which are discussed in chapter 3) does not derive, as it did as late as 1950, from a frustrated desire to work in conventionally designated "male" occupations, or from the belief that their worth or value as persons is any the less because they do not, like men, work, for example, in the wheat fields or the fruit orchards. And how different, in this regard, they are, not only from the pioneer women when the latter were their age, but also, it must be noted, from what they themselves were—those of them old enough to be in the labor force—twenty-five years ago. In 1950 the women who worked on the land, pioneers and sabras alike, had constantly to prove—to themselves, if not to others—that they were the equals of men. They never failed to impress me with the zeal, indeed the fanaticism, with which they worked. They tended to work longer than the men, they took fewer and shorter breaks, and they worked at a more strenuous pace. When I once commented on this to a sabra with whom I was working in the vegetable garden, she volunteered that her ambition was focused on her work, although, she went on to say, it was very difficult for a mother with young children (she had two) to work in the fields. But, she continued, whatever the difficulties—"sometimes it is so difficult that it does not seem worthwhile"—she had to persist because her goal was to attain social status, not any kind of status, but status as a farm worker. To achieve this goal she not only pushed herself to work during the day, but she spent her free nights studying the technical farm journals relevant to her work.

Today this obsessive concern to prove their worth as women, by demonstrating that they are as good as any man—in the things that men do—is dead. For the older sabras, it has become a historical memory; for the younger ones it is merely another of those "quaint" ideas that the pioneering generation had dreamed up. This change is especially important relative to the theoretical argument of this book because the sabras' disinterest in agricultural labor persists despite the fact that, as "productive" labor, it is the most prestigeful. Although this would be the avenue to sexual equality in its "identity" meaning, they are nevertheless not interested in pursuing it.

This dramatic change in the women's attitudes is perhaps best symbolized in the following vignette. One of the first sabras I met upon my return to Kiryat Yedidim in 1975, a rate-busting field worker when I knew her in 1950, had undergone a remarkable transformation. Angular and strident in her twenties, she had become in her forties a jolly and warm woman. Having given up her agricultural career many years ago, she was now the social worker in charge of the elderly and incapacitated, and prior to that she had worked for a number of years as a cook in the communal kitchen. Perceiving my barely disguised look of shock—others, perhaps, but not Ruth!— she went on to explain that some years ago she had come to realize how "crazy" it had been to distinguish between farm ( = important) and service ( = unimportant) work. "To feed cows or chickens was 'farm work,' hence 'good,' but to feed people was 'service work,' hence 'bad.' One day I decided that's just crazy, and that to feed people was also creative. So I went to work in the kitchen, and I loved it."

We may summarize this discussion of the changing attitudes toward sex-role differentiation by reiterating that, sometime in the quarter century between 1950 and 1975, most kibbutz women (and men too) had come to view sexual specialization in the economy as a natural and, with certain qualifications concerning the specific form it has taken in the kibbutz, a desirable state of affairs. Their attitudinal changes, moreover, are based on their changing conceptions of sexual equality. Rejecting its "identity" meaning as espoused by the pioneer women (and articulated in the kibbutz feminist ideology) they have adopted instead the "equivalence" meaning of sexual equality. Although remarkable enough, this change is but one facet of a comprehensive change ("revolution" is perhaps a better term) that has taken place in the early feminist ideology of the kibbutz. In the following sections, we shall examine the other facets of this change and the structural consequences attendant upon them.

## Governance

One of the motives, it will be recalled, for emancipating women from the yoke of domestic work was the expectation that they would thereby be able (and willing) to participate equally with men in political activities. Specifically, this meant proportional recruitment of both sexes to the leadership positions as well as to the various administrative committees that in effect organize kibbutz life, and equal participation in the general assembly, the ultimate decision-making body of the kibbutz. This expectation has not been fulfilled.

From the very beginning, some of the leadership positions of the kibbutz became male monopolies simply because women did not have the requisite knowledge for undertaking these responsibilities. Since women typically did not work in the agricultural branches of the economy, most of them did not have the experience to assume such central roles as general economic manager (*merakez meshek*) or treasurer (*gizbar*). For the same reason, the lesser position of work organizer (*merakez avodah*) became a male monopoly until, some years ago, it was decided to distribute this function between two officials, one male (for the allocation of men's work) and one female (for the allocation of women's). However, even in the branches of the economy in which women have the same expertise as men, it has been unusual for a woman to become a foreman (*merakez anaf*) except in exclusively female branches. Recently, as men have begun to work in the kitchen, even the kitchen staff (which is still primarily female) is frequently headed by a man, although collectively women have had much more experience in the kitchen than men. In noneconomic leadership roles the pattern is the same. The general secretary (*mazkir*), almost without exception, had been a male until a few years ago, when, again, it was decided to elect two persons to this position, one male and one female. According to the most recent data, 64 percent of all management positions in the

Kibbutz Artzi federation were held by men (Tiger and Shepher 1975:90).

In examining the composition of the administrative committees, the participation of women appears to be somewhat more balanced. In 1969, for example, 49 women and 63 men served on these committees in Kiryat Yedidim. But these numbers in themselves do not tell the whole story, for the distribution of committee assignments reveals that the sex-role differentiation found in the economy has pervaded the entire social structure. Thus, the secretariat, the central decision-making organ, comprises nine men and only four women; the finance committee, which allocates economic resources among the economic branches, and determines the relative distribution of resources to savings, investment, and consumption, consists of eight men and only one woman. Moreover, the committees on work, military security, physical plant maintenance, garage and equipment, and basketball have no women at all. On the other hand, some committees have a preponderantly female membership, and this, again, reflects the changing conceptions of appropriate female activities. Thus, the child care committee has nine women and only two men; the library committee, two women and one man; the high school committee, four women and one man; the health committee, three women and one man; the clothing committee, six women and only two men.

A few years ago, the leadership of Kibbutz Artzi, alarmed by the disproportionately low participation of women in kibbutz governance, commissioned a study of this "problem." Its findings with respect to this entire federation are entirely consistent with those I have described for Kiryat Yedidim, as Table 1 indicates. This study

*Table 1.* Distribution of women in governance in Kibbutz Artzi.

| nonactive | 64% |
|-----------|-----|
| service   | 10  |
| social    | 8   |
| education | 7   |
| cultural  | 6   |
| general   | 3   |
| economic  | 3   |

*Note*—This table is reworked from Anonymous 1969:19.

also discovered that, parallel to the situation in Kiryat Yedidim, women in all kibbutzim attend the general assembly less frequently and participate less actively than men.

Women are not only underrepresented in administrative committees, but as is also true of the economy, they infrequently assume leadership roles in the committees on which they serve. Thus, the above study of Kibbutz Artzi revealed that only 2 percent of the women serve as chairmen of service committees, 1 percent of economic committees, and less than 1 percent of social and education committees. Hence, women rarely serve as chairmen even for those committees on which they constitute a majority.

The underrepresentation of women in kibbutz governance holds for extra-kibbutz political and leadership activities, as well. Thus for the entire federation, males comprise 84 percent of the participants in economic public service, 71 percent of the leadership positions of the federation, and 78 percent of the political activists (Tiger and Shepher 1975:91).

These various findings, it should be added, have been replicated in other studies of individual kibbutzim (Shain 1974) and of other kibbutz federations (Talmon-Garber 1965). Indeed, one of the federations, worried by the low frequency of female participation in kibbutz governance, went so far as to require that women comprise at least one-third of the membership of its administrative committees and other governing bodies. Even this standard, however, was seldom attained because, despite this ruling, few women were willing to serve.

This last sentence contains the explanation for all the other findings related to the role of women in kibbutz governance. As in the case of their small proportion in farming, only a few women occupy leadership positions in kibbutz governance because the majority are not interested. Moreover, the typical explanation which they offer for sex-role differentiation in the political system is the same explanation they adduce for its prevalence in the economic system, viz., men and women have different interests. Women (according to the majority of both males and females in our six-kibbutz sample) tend to be more concerned with their families, while men, even family-oriented men, are more concerned with communitywide affairs. In Kiryat Yedidim this view was also found in 1950, but then it was held by a minority.

This is not the only explanation they offer for the small proportion of politically active women. Many women say that they are uncomfortable in positions of authority and responsibility, whether political or economic, which is why the chairmen of committees, even those in which women are a majority, are usually males. Responsibility for an administrative committee or a branch of the economy usually causes them a degree of stress or tension that they would prefer to avoid. Correlatively, some women wish to avoid economic branches headed by other women, claiming that they are characterized by greater conflict and tension than those headed by men.

It is clear, then, that neither a culture that has stressed the importance of political leadership and participation on the part of women, nor a social system that has encouraged and facilitated this end, has had its intended consequences. It should be emphasized, moreover, that the attitudes of the sabra men—those at least who comprised our six-kibbutz sample—are highly favorable to the notion of female leadership. To be sure, some of the men expressed reservations, if not opposition, to female leadership in such central economic positions as general manager and treasurer. The great majority, however, said that they favored the recruitment of women even to these positions, assuming that they were qualified, and not one among this majority entertained any doubts about women being intellectually qualified for these posts. Rather, they attributed the women's infrequent recruitment to these positions to motivational and temperamental variables, especially—while the women are still young—to their greater concern with family and children.

In order to put this discussion in proper perspective, it should be noted that few of the elective offices in the kibbutz, except for those of general secretary, general manager, and treasurer, are full-time positions. The responsibilities demanded of all the other offices must be undertaken after working hours and since there are few rewards associated with these responsibilities, many men are only slightly less reluctant than women to assume the burdens of office. Nevertheless, many more men than women are willing, or can be cajoled, to accept leadership positions, especially those of an economic nature. And this generalization holds even for those men whose family interests are no less strong than their female counterparts. Moreover, to the extent that women are motivated, or can be induced to assume central leadership roles, the latter almost always relate to social, cultural, and educational concerns.

In short, if kibbutz governance has become predominantly male, it is not because of lack of opportunity for, or encouragement of women, but because most of them—there are, of course, many exceptions—are not interested in acquiring positions of authority and leadership. Their lack of interest is markedly discrepant from both the conception of female emancipation held by the feminist ideology of the kibbutz and its analysis of the means by which this goal might be achieved. This ideology, it will be recalled, viewed the political activization of women as one of the goals of female emancipation, for sexual equality required the abolition of sex-role differentiation in the polity no less than in the economy. This goal could only be achieved, it was assumed, by the liberation of women from family ties and domestic responsibilities, for only then could they find the motivation and the energy to participate in political life. It was to this end (among others) that the kibbutz instituted its changes in the traditional marriage and family systems.

For the kibbutz ideologists, therefore, it was all the more disappointing (and surprising) that the changes introduced in the traditional marriage and family systems did not produce the political consequences they anticipated. Their disappointment, however, does not necessarily mean that the ideology was wrong in viewing the women's emotional involvement in the family as an obstacle to their development of political motivation. It might be suggested, rather, that it was wrong in underestimating the strength of this involvement. This, at least, is the lesson of hindsight, as we shall see in the next two sections.

## Marriage

Although to a large extent kibbutz marriage today is little different from what it was in 1950, it has nevertheless reverted in some important respects to its traditional structural form and cultural importance. Symbolic of this reversal is the restoration of the traditional terms of reference for the spouse. Although, in 1950, the occasional woman would lapse into "my husband" in referring to her spouse, the norm was still "my friend" or "my man." Today, "my husband" is used by all women, including the most radical of the early feminists, and they use it neither with self-consciousness, nor (as I first thought) with irony. Indeed, when I twitted one of the feminists about this, she was unaware of the change that I was calling to her attention. This return to a traditional idiom most certainly does not reflect a change in the status of the kibbutz wife from an equal to a subordinate partner, but it does reflect the fact that marriage has again become (for males and females alike) a very important institution.

Perhaps the most important symbol of this counterrevolution is the return to the traditional wedding and the public celebration of marriage. In the early kibbutz, marriage was legitimized simply by the granting of a joint room to the couple; any public celebration was studiously avoided. If the couple subsequently decided to formalize their union by a legal ceremony, it was only after deciding to have children; and even then, many couples would dramatize their contempt for the religious ceremony—a civil ceremony cannot be obtained in Israel—by appearing before the rabbi only after the wife was obviously pregnant. In any event, this ceremony (*chatuna*) was taken as neither the sign nor the symbol of the union, and (as might be expected) it was never held in the kibbutz. In Kiryat Yedidim it was not until 1950, during my original study of this kibbutz, that the first break in the dam occurred. A sabra couple, wishing (so they claimed) to escape the derision they anticipated during their year's study in Jerusalem, decided to legalize their two-year-old marriage by performing a traditional ceremony, following which their parents arranged a public reception in their honor. To celebrate a marriage publicly was, in those days, bad enough; but to celebrate it on the day of the chatuna, as if the latter (rather than its sanction by the kibbutz) constituted its legitimation, was nothing short of scandalous.

But the scandal of the past has become the norm for the present. Today, every marriage is the occasion for a public and elaborate reception; the marriage is officially announced and the couple and their parents congratulated in the kibbutz weekly newspaper; most important, it is the chatuna, which occurs when the couple decides to marry, that is taken as the sign and symbol of the marriage, and it is after this ceremony takes place that the reception is held. The magnitude of this change may be gauged by the fact that of the sixty subjects in our six-kibbutz survey, not even one understood why they were asked to comment on the reasons for solemnizing kibbutz marriages by means of a wedding ceremony. The typical response to our question was: "How does this question relate uniquely to the kibbutz? Weddings are performed in the kibbutz for the same reasons they are performed anywhere else." Not one of these sabras seemed to be aware of the revolutionary attitudes toward marriage that were reflected in this answer.

But this is not all. In Kiryat Yedidim, at least, yet another barrier was broken in 1975 when a couple invited the rabbi to perform their wedding in the kibbutz. Their motive seemed reasonable enough: the bride was from the city, and the innovation was in deference to her parents. Still, it would not have been reason enough in the past, as one of the pioneers (she who saw no objection to the use of "husband") complained bitterly.

Given this change in the attitude to the wedding ceremony, it will come as no surprise to learn that the other attempts of the kibbutz founders to minimize the importance of the marriage relationship—by the couple refraining from showing affection in public, or from sitting together in public, or, more generally, by avoiding any public behavior that might symbolize their union—these attempts, which were already being discarded in 1950, have been totally abandoned.

With the renewed importance of the marriage bond, the marital residence has acquired increasing importance. The unit of consumption has shifted from the group to the married couple (or, more properly, the domestic family), and this has been accompanied by a dramatic increase in the budget allocated by the kibbutz for housing, as well as for furniture, clothing, and a variety of other consumer goods which in the past would either have been entirely inaccessible, or else available only in communal institutions (such as the kibbutz dining room) or in public places (such as the clubhouse). Thus, for example, housing has evolved over the years from a tent, to a one-room wooden shack, to a room-and-a-half studio apartment, and, finally, to a two-and-a-half room apartment. And this impressive development in both the size and the quality of the family residence has been accompanied by an equally impressive development in its contents. Public showers and toilets (which were still the norm in 1950) have been replaced by private bathrooms, and the electric teakettle (which was still objected to in 1950) has been replaced by a full kitchen (equipped with refrigerator and stove). Central heating and air conditioning, not even imagined in 1950, are found in every apartment, as are a radio, a stereo, and a television set. In short, the marital residence, which was originally conceived as a necessary, but temporary, retreat from public institutions and places where life was "really" lived—after all, one did have to rest and sleep—has become the focus of the couple's life.

These material changes, to be sure, are a consequence of the remarkable economic success of the kibbutz, and the abandonment of its early ascetic ideology. But the decision to allocate public resources for the private consumption of the married couple, rather than for collective consumption in communal institutions, reflects the dramatic change in the cultural importance of marriage and (as we shall see) of the family that has occurred over the past twenty-five years. Concommitant with this change there has occurred an increasing privatization of the married couple which, already noticeable in 1950, has developed to a much greater degree since then. The private apartment, rather than the communal dining room, has bcome the locus of the couple's social life. It is there (with its radio, stereo, and TV) that they find their entertainment. It is there, too, that their children have been increasingly spending more of their time. (Indeed, the growing importance of the family is at least an equally important reason for this increasing privatization, as well as for the reallocation of kibbutz resources from the public to the private domain.)

With the increasing importance of marriage, the life of a bachelor has become all but untenable. As one informant put it, "To be a bachelor in the kibbutz is impossible." Discounting for the obvious hyperbole, the intent of this statement is clear. As couples spend more of their time together and (as we shall see) with their children, bachelors feel increasingly isolated and excluded from the social life of the families. Even when they are included, the results are not entirely satisfactory; the married couples are absorbed in their children, which the bachelor finds boring, and his concerns, in turn, are of little interest to them.

This is one, but not the only reason—since it holds for Israel in general—that marriage in the kibbutz occurs at a relatively early age. For females, especially, to remain unmarried is a "tragedy" (although the kibbutz social system has destroyed any economic basis for such a view), and the young woman of twenty-five who is not yet married is an object both of pity and concern (although kibbutz sexual morality does not preclude sexual gratification outside of marriage). It is little wonder that such women increasingly leave the kibbutz to seek a life (and husband) in the city.

With this increasing social and cultural importance of marriage, there has ensued an important change in the attitude to divorce. In the early days of the kibbutz, divorce (as might have been expected from the attitude towards marriage) was entirely permissive, and although as early as 1950 the divorce rate had already undergone a sharp decline, the permissive attitude itself had undergone little change. Since then, the divorce rate has not only continued to decline—from 7 percent for the first generation to 4 percent for the younger generations in the Kibbutz Artzi federation, a decline of almost 50 percent—but also the attitude to divorce has changed from a permissive to a negative one. Today, public opinion is actively opposed to divorce. Although not viewed as immoral, it is certainly viewed as unfortunate—and not a few parents of divorced couples view it as humiliating and tragic—and the kibbutz makes every effort to keep the couple together. As a consequence, unhappy couples, who formerly would have separated, remain married. In one of the kibbutzim we studied, for example, a couple that was on the verge of divorce (because the wife was having an affair) was sent on a two-year foreign mission with the hope that their trip might cement their fragile marriage. The latter example points to the changing attitude to extramarital affairs which, not unexpectedly, has accompanied the changing attitude to divorce. In the early years affairs were viewed by the kibbutz with the same permissive attitude with which it viewed divorce. Although today only a few sabras criticize them as intrinsically immoral, most of the subjects in our six-kibbutz sample were nevertheless opposed to affairs if they were disruptive of the marriage.

Although these changes in the kibbutz attitudes to marriage characterize both sexes, they appear to be stronger in women than in men. Thus, adverting to the problem of divorce, the former appear to be the more vigorous in their general opposition to divorce, just as in any particular case it is the wife who seems to be especially concerned about the dissolution of the marriage. The most frequent explanation offered for this new attitude, however, relates not so much to a concern for the welfare of the spouses as for that of their children. It is the latter, so it is alleged, who would suffer the most from the dissolution of the marriage. This concern with the integrity of the family brings us to the last change to be discussed here.

## Family

According to the feminist ideology of the kibbutz, it will be recalled, the woman's involvement in the family was seen as the major obstacle to female emancipation. By freeing the mother from domestic cares and concerns, and by enabling her to work full time outside the domestic household, the kibbutz pioneers expected that for the woman, no less than for the man, the family would be superseded by work as the focus of her life. Although this expectation seems to have been realized (at least in part) in the early years of kibbutz history, today the family has once again acquired for most women a position of affective centrality in their lives. By contrast, although the family is also important for the man, work continues to be the dominant interest for the majority.

In a recent public opinion survey in Kibbutz Artzi, in which the respondents were asked to rank the relative importance of work, family, public activities, study, and hobbies, most men ranked work, while most women ranked family, as first in importance (Leviatan 1975:23). Surprisingly enough the female rebels (now old women) of the pioneering generation were no different in this regard from their sabra daughters and granddaughters. Similar findings were obtained by Shain (1974:174–76, 208–9) in an anthropological study of a single kibbutz, not affiliated with Kibbutz Artzi. In contrast to the men, the majority of the women in this kibbutz claimed that they were more involved in the family than in work, and much more dependent upon it for personal fulfillment. Moreover, like the Kibbutz Artzi study, Shain found that the sabra women were more involved with their families than the pioneer women were. For the pioneering generation, 68 percent of the women, compared with 32 percent of the men, considered their roles as spouse and parent to be more important than their role as worker. For the second generation, the difference between men and women was even more pronounced: 88 percent of the women, compared with 27 percent of the men, considered their family roles to be more important.

Lest these findings be misinterpreted, it should be stressed that they refer to relative, not absolute, emphases. Interviews from our six-kibbutz samples indicate that men (and women too) who rank work higher than family may still be deeply involved in the family and importantly concerned with their children and their welfare. The difference is that the latter are not their focal concern, whereas the converse is the case among those men and women who rank the family higher. And although the kibbutz studied by Shain may be somewhat extreme in the magnitude of the discrepancy between male and female attitudes, all studies (including my six-kibbutz study) indicate that family and children occupy a central place in the emotional concerns of a much larger percentage of sabra women than of sabra men. This holds not only for those women who are discontented with their work (and from whom such attitudes are expectable) but also for those who like their work. Consider the following response of a highly talented thirty-year-old woman, presently a bookkeeper in one of these kibbutzim, when asked whether her family or her work was more important to her: "What a question! The family is more important than anything. Look, my work is extremely important to me. I want very much to work, but I wouldn't invest one-fourth the thought to my work that I invest in my family, under no circumstances."

Although these findings are based on recent studies, the phenomena which they report are not at all recent; they merely confirm what has been known within the kibbutz movement itself for at least twenty-five years. Thus, in the 1950 pronouncement (quoted in chapter 1) which claimed the kibbutz had emancipated women from the shackles that had chained their hands, the authors go on to say that their structural emancipation had not achieved its expected psychological emancipation: ". . . we forgot that their hands had been chained for hundreds of years, [and] that an organ which does not function for such a long time becomes paralyzed."

That the family was becoming a central interest of the women as early as the fifties was also reported as a research finding in two independent investigations (Spiro 1955, Talmon-Garber 1956). Nevertheless, there is an important difference between the family orientation of the women of 1950 and those of 1975, as the data from Kiryat Yedidim indicate. Although the pioneers, in 1950, were clearly ambivalent about their involvement in their families, many sabras were even then resolving their ambivalence by beginning to

accept the fact that the family provided their most important gratifications. Most of the pioneers were disdainful of the sabra attitude,
which they characterized as a "petit-bourgeois retreat." Their disdain
was typified in the following comment. "They [the sabras] have
closed their doors to the outside world, and have become typical
*balebostes* [old-fashioned housewives]." This nascent trend of 1950
has become the norm of 1975. Most married women, both young
and old, are deeply committed to their newly cathected roles as
housewives and mothers. Activities which would have seemed un-
believable for a kibbutz woman a generation ago—baking pies and
cakes for the family, crocheting sweaters for her children, preparing
breakfast for them in the family apartment on her day off and dinner
on Saturday evening—these, and more, are now typical female
activities.

To put it somewhat more abstractly, instead of being viewed as
an obstacle to female emancipation, the care of and concern for their
children is now viewed by many women as an important source of
personal fulfillment. What is more, many perceive their maternal
orientation as biologically determined, or, to use their term, as "natural." This reversal of the cultural determinism of the early kibbutz
ideology may sometimes be rather dramatic, as the following quota-
tions (the first from a pioneer woman, the second from a young
sabra) indicate:

I feel that female physiology and psychology are different from
those of the male because of the woman's child-bearing role. A
woman feels she is the center of the family; in fact, she makes
the family what it is. She cannot give up this position. She does
not want to give up this position. Therefore, generation after
generation, a type has evolved; the woman has become psychologically different from the man.

Although the sexes may have the same abilities in art and
science, men are usually superior because women are so absorbed in their basic responsibilities of child and home care.
Everything she is and has is devoted to this—her joys, her
thoughts, her nerves. It is the most important thing in the world
to her. This is a natural feeling for women—to want to create
children and a stable family life. It is a feeling of fulfillment. To
give life is to overcome death. (Shain 1974:215)

The above are the opinions of some typical women in an established kibbutz belonging to a nonradical federation. As an index of culture change, the following statement by a women's rights leader of the more radical Kibbutz Artzi federation is much more significant.

As for the essence of equality between man and woman—we cannot ignore the fact that there is not only a physiological difference, but there are also emotional differences that influence the attitudes and way of life of the woman even in the kibbutz, and therefore there is no ignoring the special familial functions of the female comrade. (Amirah Sartani, in Anonymous 1974:5)

The female sabras' unashamed view of children as a form of self-fulfillment is the most important reason for the increase in the Kibbutz birth rate over the past quarter century. A generation ago, not one couple in Kiryat Yedidim, for example, had more than two children. Today, three and four are typical, while five and even six are not unheard of. One informant, highly critical of the attitudes of the younger sabra women, commented: "All they want to do is make babies; they have no interest in anything else." This, of course, is typical sabra hyperbole, but it does serve to underscore the important change that has occurred in the women's involvement with children.

Sabra women not only have more children than their mothers, but they want to spend more time with them and to assume a greater role in their care. Although this desire was just as strong among many women twenty-five years ago (not only among the sabras, but among their mothers as well), the changes they had then desired in the structure of collective socialization had gone unheeded. Today, however, almost all kibbutzim (including Kiryat Yedidim) have implemented most of them. Thus, for example, instead of placing her new baby in the infants' house upon returning from the hospital, the mother keeps it in her apartment for the first six weeks, and, if she chooses, she may have it sleep in her apartment up to eight months. Again, in addition to the afternoon visit in their apartment with their preschool children, mothers may now leave their work in midmorning in order to visit with them (either in the play yard or in their apartment) for an hour or so. This visit, symbolically enough, is called the "hour of love" (*she'at ahava*). Moreover, mothers (and fathers, too) feel entirely free to visit the children's houses whenever they have the time, without being made to feel (as was often the case in the past) like unwelcome intruders. Perhaps, however, the most dramatic change has occurred in the duration of the children's afternoon visit in the parents' apartment. In the past, this visit was typically confined to two hours, from about 4:00 P.M. (when the parents returned from work) till about 6:00 P.M. (when the children returned for their evening meal in the children's houses). Today, however, the visit extends from four to five hours (depending on the child's age.) Instead of eating in the children's houses, the children, beginning with the first grade, have their evening meal with their parents in the kibbutz dining room, and they do not return to the children's houses until it is time for bed at 8:00 or 9:00 P.M. Moreover, instead of visiting with their parents for only a few hours on Saturday (as was done in the past), children today spend almost the entire day in their parents' apartments, and (usually together with their grandparents) they eat their evening meal there as well. Finally, the pressing problem of *hashkava* (preparing the child for sleep) has also been resolved. Seemingly a minor issue, by 1950 the frustration felt by many mothers at leaving their child for the nurse to prepare for bed was experienced as the thwarting of a vital maternal need, as well as a symbol of all their accumulating resentments concerning the physical separation from their children. By 1975 the older system of hashkava had been changed: today, parents rather than nurses are entrusted with this responsibility.

All these changes were resisted and many of them are still severely criticized by many pioneers who view them as violation of the early values of the kibbutz ideology for which they had fought so hard. But that is not their only complaint. The influx of children into the dining room, to take a specific example, has raised the general noise level and confusion, with the result (they complain) that they no longer enjoy their evening meal. The consequence of these changes, one pioneer predicted, will be that within five years no one will take his dinner in the dining room, and instead, evening meals will be cooked and eaten by each family in its apartment. When this happens, she continued, the kibbutz will have taken the final step from its evolution (as she sees it) from a collective (*kibbutz*) to a cooperative (*moshav shitufi*) social system.

Although for the more conservative pioneers the attempts of the kibbutz to meet the mothers' maternal needs have already gone too far, for many sabras they have not gone far enough. For the latter, these needs will not be fully satisfied until the present sleeping arrangements are changed so that children can sleep with their parents rather than in the children's houses. Actually, as we shall see below, the latter sleeping arrangement has been the primary cause of many women's discontent with collective socialization from the very beginning. That the pioneer women, however, did not press for changes in the system reflected, among other things, their conviction that their commitment to female emancipation must take precedence over their maternal sentiments. Hence, by 1950, in Kiryat Yedidim at least, the major proponents of change were not the pioneer women but a younger generation of mothers who had joined the kibbutz some fifteen years after its founding, and whose ideological commitments were less strong than those of the pioneers. On the other hand, sabra mothers, with some few exceptions, were entirely content with these sleeping arrangements, not from ideological motives, however, but from pragmatic ones. They enjoyed the freedom it allowed them. By 1975, however, the exception had become the rule, and it is among the younger sabras—for, of course, by 1975 all kibbutz mothers are second generation, or young first generation sabras—that the desire for this change from "collective sleeping" (*lina meshutefet*) to "family sleeping" (*lina mishpachtit*) is especially strong.

Although the proponents of family sleeping feel strongly about this issue, their percentage is difficult to assess. In the six-kibbutz survey that I conducted in 1976, 55 percent of the sabra women preferred family sleeping, 27 percent preferred collective sleeping, and 18 percent were undecided. For the sabra men, the preferences were reversed: 37 percent preferred family sleeping, 42 percent preferred collective sleeping, and 21 percent were undecided.[2]

2. In this survey, the differences among the three kibbutz federations were negligible. Since, however, the number of respondents of each sex from each of the federations was small, interkibbutz comparisons are not entirely reliable. In a survey conducted in 1969 of 900 kibbutz sabras (Anonymous 1971), the differences among the federations were impressive. Thus, while in the Kibbutz Artzi federation, 12 percent of the male and 25 percent of the female sabras favored the change (compared to 7 percent of the male and 14 percent of the female pioneers), the percentages in the other two federations were dramatically higher. In the Kibbutz Meuchad federation, the percentages for male and female sabras, respectively, were 29 and 56 percent; in the Ichud federation they reach 41 and 70 percent. In my judgment, however, the true percentage for the sabras in Kibbutz Artzi was much higher than the figures indicate because (as the auth-

Bowing to this desire, more than three-fourths of the kibbutzim of one federation (the *Ichud*) have instituted the change from collective to family sleeping. Most kibbutzim, including those in which a majority favor this change, have not followed their lead for at least two reasons. First, the kibbutz establishment is opposed to changes in the socialization system of the kibbutz on ideological grounds. In effect, "family sleeping" means a return to the domestic household, and the latter is viewed as a violation of a fundamental element of kibbutz ideology. As one leader put it: "The kibbutz has undergone many changes, and despite the dire warnings, the kibbutz did not 'come to an end.' But this change ['family sleeping'] would constitute a serious blow to the fundamental character of the kibbutz."

The sabras, whose commitment to ideology is minimal, are not persuaded by such arguments. Their opposition to the change to family sleeping, even when it is a majority preference, is economic. Having already made a major economic investment both in the children's houses and the adult apartments, the capital outlay required for remodeling the apartments would be prohibitive. A highly respected male sabra of Kiryat Yedidim who, like most males, is content with the present system, expressed the prevailing view (of both sexes). "I know" he said, "that many mothers are unhappy in the kibbutz because of 'collective sleeping,' and although I personally prefer this arrangement, if it would make them happy I would certainly be willing to change to 'family sleeping.' But at the moment, the subject is academic. We simply do not have the financial resources to make this change."

For our present purpose, the desire for change, taken as a measure of the women's maternal needs, is as important as change itself, and in documenting the strength of these needs, it is important to understand the reasons for their discontent with the present sleeping arrangement. Some of the reasons one hears today are the same as those heard in 1950 (which in turn go as far back as the twenties);

---

ors of the survey themselves observe) the expressed preference of the respondents was influenced to a large extent by the prevailing formal ideology of their respective federations, and Kibbutz Artzi was the federation which formally was most committed to the original kibbutz ideology. This ideological influence is reflected in the large percentage of the total sample (28 percent) who expressed themselves as undecided. Whatever the true percentage, it should be noted that those who favored the change felt so strongly about this issue that it was one of the most important causes for leaving the kibbutz (Rosner, in Anonymous 1974:22).

other reasons, however, are new. Today, as in 1950, mothers complain about the emotional difficulty of parting with their children at night, of their anxiety about leaving them without a resident adult, of their concern over children's night fears that result from or cannot be allayed when they sleep apart from them.[3] But demographic and ecological changes in the kibbutz have added new complaints. Today, the parents' apartments are much farther from the children's houses, and it is most unpleasant to go out on cold and rainy evenings to put the children to sleep. Moreover, for those women who work in child care and who have many children of their own the present system is often conducive to both chaos and rage. The evening meal is gulped down in order to get a younger child to bed on time, following which there is a rush to another children's house to supervise the children in their professional care, and then the rush to yet another children's house to put an elder child to bed, and so on.

As important as these reasons may be, the main reason for the women wanting their children with them at night relates to their maternal needs; in the present system, they contend, they are not fulfilled as mothers. The following comment, by a sabra mother in her twenties, sums it up: "When the mother returns to her apartment after she has put her child to bed, she feels that something is lacking. Something is lacking, too, when she cannot awaken her child in the morning and watch him open his eyes. The mother wishes to begin the morning in a family framework. . . . She wants the child with her because that is how her maternal feelings are fulfilled."

It was almost uncanny to hear young mothers express these sentiments in 1975 because I had heard almost identical sentiments expressed by their grandmothers in 1950. Let me cite but one example. A pioneer woman, then in her early fifties, was in charge of her grandson while her son and daughter-in-law were on vacation. Most of his classmates being ill at the time, the grandson slept the night in her apartment. She had not slept the entire night, the grandmother told me, thinking how "thrilling" it would be the next morning to

3. In the 1950s, and going back to the early days of the kibbutz, a night watch made the rounds of the children's houses to make sure that all was in order. If a child was frightened or needed something, the night watch could then attend to his or her needs. In some few instances, the parent of a child suffering from night terrors might sleep for a time in the children's house. Recently, this system has been augmented by a central electronic switchboard connected to each children's house. If a child is frightened or has some need, he need only sound the buzzer to bring the required adult assistance.

awaken and find her grandson with her. This woman was an intellectual and a strong feminist, and that neither she nor her contemporaries opposed the system of "collective sleeping" when they were the age of this sabra mother was more a reflection of their commitment to the antifamilistic tenet of their feminist ideology than of a weak emotional attachment to their children. For them, as we have seen, female emancipation required the attenuation of the mother-child bond and the exercise of restraint in the display of maternal affection.

How conflicted they must have been, however, as young mothers in the 1920s can be gauged by their own testimony. Two examples will suffice. In 1975, reminiscing about the early days of Kiryat Yedidim, a grandmother described how as a young mother she would take her children at night to the children's house, and however much they cried when she left, she would not return. "But," she continued in a tone of half-regret and half-apology, "it was very difficult, very difficult." More poignant still is the following passage, written by a young mother fifty years ago, who recorded her feelings while she experienced them.

> Is it right to make the child return for the night to the children's home, to say goodnight to it and send it back to sleep among the fifteen or twenty others? This parting from the child before sleep is so unjust! . . . The women on the night watch in the children's homes take turn and turn about. And when my turn comes to "go on guard" I feel my heart contract every time a child calls out in the night—sometimes out of its sleep, not knowing what it is calling—"Night sister! Night sister [night watch]!" What is taking place in the soul of the child at that moment, between sleeping and waking? And who knows what is more important for the child, the conscious life of the day or the unconscious life of the night? (A.T., in Shazar 1975:206)

It seems fair to conclude that the changes observed in the sabras' maternal behavior reflect a historical change not in the maternal feelings of kibbutz women, but in the freedom they experience to express them. Having rejected the pioneers' conception of female emancipation, with its "identity" meaning of sexual equality, sabra women neither experience a sense of incompatibility between a commitment to both motherhood and emancipation, nor is their self-image as emancipated women threatened by the fact that family roles have not acquired as central a position for men as they have for them. Indeed, the most important change that has occurred in the family attitudes of some kibbutz men is their increasing perception of women as the latter have increasingly come to perceive themselves, namely, primarily as mothers and wives. Thus, in the kibbutz studied by Shain (1974:201) twenty-one of twenty-five pioneer men, and thirteen of fifteen sabra men, conceived of women most importantly as mother and wife, and only secondarily as worker.

From its very inception, the kibbutz has been a child-oriented society, par excellence. Indeed, one of its ultimate goals was the raising up of a new generation of children who would come to embody the characteristics of the "new man," whose creation was the very raison d'etre of the kibbutz enterprise. Hence, from the very beginning, the concern with children had always been a focus of kibbutz activity, and more resources—of time, energy, capital, thought, labor, affect—have been invested in their care and development than in any other kibbutz activity. If, then, there has been a revolutionary change in the women's attitudes to children—and, in this regard, in the men's as well—this change consists of a radical shift (at least normatively) from a universalistic attachment to the children of the kibbutz to a particularistic attachment to one's own children.

To gauge this change, one need only contrast the particularistic parent-child sentiments described in the preceding discussion with the situation that obtained at the beginning of kibbutz history. In those early days, every child born in the kibbutz was to be viewed (by his parents, as well as by the kibbutz) not so much as belonging to his parents as to the kibbutz. "What we consider of importance," wrote a pioneer woman (Nina Richter, in Shazar 1975:194), "is the *inner* attitude of the group and of every individual comrade toward the children and the inner feeling of responsibility toward every newborn child." To be sure, this "inner feeling" was not easy to achieve— "We have not," Richter continued, "reached the final stage in which the children belong to the group as a whole"—but it was nevertheless the ideal to which to aspire. Hence, children were referred to not only as so-and-so's children, but as "our children." It was because they were "our children" that the practice (described in a previous section) of a mother nursing another's baby in order to equalize the weight of all babies, was viewed by the mothers as desirable if not entirely natural. For the same reason, when a baby was born to any couple it was as though a baby had been born to the kibbutz, and it was the kibbutz, its extended family as it were, that was to be congratulated. Today, although the entire kibbutz is still invited to the celebration for the birth of a baby, it is the parents who arrange the celebration, and it is they (and their parents) who are toasted and congratulated.

As a result of this psychological change from a universalistic to a particularistic orientation to children (a change which, as we have seen, has been less affective, however, than normative), there have ensued important structural changes in the kibbutz. Whereas in its early history, the kibbutz could be described as a child-oriented social system, today it is best described as a social system comprised of child-oriented families. In short, as a result of the particularization of the parent-child bond, there has been a structural reversal in the figure-ground relationship of family and kibbutz. In the early days, the kibbutz itself could be conceived as an undifferentiated family; today the family can be conceived as a differentiated structure within the kibbutz.

This generic structural change has in turn promoted other more specific changes. In the first place, it has obviously affected the collective rearing of children. In its original conception the children's house was a means not only for freeing the mother for extradomestic work, but for fostering the child's identification with the collectivity rather than his family. Normatively, that collectivity was the "children's society" (chevrat ye'ladim), which constituted, as it were, a distinctive corporate group with its own self-governance. Today, with the emphasis on the family as a structural unit, the children's house is more like a boarding school which, though still a means for freeing the mother, is no longer intended to replace the family as the focus of the child's identifications.

Second, the renewed emphasis on the family has inevitably affected the character of kibbutz social relations. In the past, as "children of the kibbutz," all children enjoyed equal status as siblings, so to speak, in a large extended family. Today, however, as children of their respective domestic families, the relative status of each family is bound to influence the manner in which others relate to them. Thus, for example, when Rivka, a teen-age girl, was criticized for a certain action, for which her peers were exempt from criticism, her mother observed that this was only natural because, "after all, Rivka is a member of *our* family, and we have a certain status here."

In this case, it should be emphasized, "our family" does not refer to Rivka's nuclear, but to her extended, family, which points to the most important structural change attendant upon the legitimation of the family as a structural unit. For the latter change is part of, and has contributed to, a more generic process, viz., the evolution of kinship relations and kinship units in the kibbutz. Almost totally absent in the past, the development of kinship sentiments has resulted in the consolidation and structuralization of bilateral kinship ties, including the formation of bilateral descent groups (which, following the Arab model, are designated by the Arabic term, *chamula.*)

Most important, in this regard, has been the institutionalization of the extended family. What I observed in its nascent form in 1950 —the children constituting a common interest for the bringing of parents and grandparents together—has now become a mature institution. If afternoon tea is frequently the informal setting for the meeting of the three-generation family in the home of the parents, high tea on Saturday afternoon has become the formal occasion for their gathering—usually, and alternately, at the homes of the respective grandparents. And if, from the discussion of changes in the maternal attitudes of kibbutz women, it might have been inferred that these changes have been restricted to the sabras, this inference must now be corrected. For if one wishes to understand the meaning of "maternal affection," one must witness its lavish expression bestowed by these grandmothers—the very women who had steeled themselves from expressing much affection for their children—on their grandchildren. (Sometimes, indeed, one can observe a dimension of rivalry between mother and daughter, or daughter-in-law, for the attention, if not affection, of the child.) As one kibbutz woman, speaking however with a tone of detachment, observed: "These grandmothers are expressing all those natural feelings which they had suppressed when they were mothers, and they were supposed to view their children as belonging to the kibbutz. Now that their daughters and granddaughters are saying, 'Nonsense, my children are mine,' these pioneers agree with them." Hence, she went on to say, "many of these women live for their grandchildren, with whom they can be the mothers they were not permitted—or did not permit themselves —to be."

With the growing importance of the extended family, there are even signs in some kibbutzim of the development of extended family households. Thus, on one kibbutz in our six-kibbutz sample, two-storey apartment units have been built, the elderly parents living in an apartment on the ground floor, and one of their married children living in the apartment on the top floor. Although each apartment is complete and separate, there is an adjoining door by which access is available from one to the other.[4]

## Femininity

A woman's self-conception as a mother and wife is inevitably related, of course, to her more general conception of herself as a woman. It should come as no surprise, therefore, that in this regard as well the sabra women have overturned the values of the pioneers. Having rejected the assumption that equality with males means becoming like males, they have also rejected its corollary (held by their grandmothers) that sexual dimorphism must be minimized as much as possible. Of course, the repudiation of the corollary had already been evident in 1951, when renewed interest in "feminine" clothing was manifested by the pioneer women themselves. But by 1975 this trend, like so many others that were evident in 1951, had become a completed revolution.

Sabra women have not only adopted feminine dress, but they are actively concerned with feminine fashion, and with sexually attractive and chic clothing. Today one sees well-cut dresses, formfitting slacks, nylon stockings, high heels, and all the accoutrement associated with a concern for femininity: jewelry, cosmetics, perfume, coiffed hair, and the like. Indeed, to fulfill these hard-won feminine

4. Shortly after my 1951 study of Kiryat Yedidim, I published a paper (Spiro 1954) in which I argued that by a prominent definition of the "family," based on a large sample of human societies (Murdock 1949:1), the family could be said to be absent from the kibbutz. Since, according to this inductive definition, the "family" is (among other things) a residential group in which parents are primarily responsible for the socialization of the children, and since the kibbutz arrangements did not satisfy these two criteria, my argument seemed reasonable. A few years later, however, I decided (Spiro 1960) that this may have been a hasty conclusion since by other, equally useful, definitions, which employed psychological rather than sociological criteria, the "family" could most certainly be said to exist in the kibbutz. Although the latter view, in my judgment, is the more cogent characterization of the situation as I observed it in 1951, the recent developments described here indicate that the parent-child group in the kibbutz is increasingly manifesting the characteristics of a "family," even when defined by the sociological criteria of coresidence and socialization.

interests, the kibbutz now has a beauty parlor, complete with beauticians, a skin specialist, and a masseuse. The notion that a woman would not try to enhance her beauty, but would even go out of her way to conceal it, is another one of those "crazy" attitudes of their grandmothers that sabra females view with unconcealed amazement.

The sabra concern with femininity, however, is not restricted to their interest in a feminine appearance. For most of them it also includes, as we have already seen, domesticity—what some of the pioneer women characterize disdainfully as a return to the Jewish mother (*Yiddishe mamma*) or the devoted housewife (*baleboste*) syndrome. However it be characterized, the syndrome is hardly restricted to the sabras, for most pioneer women manifest it as well. Two characteristics are especially prominent: a renewed interest in cooking and baking (especially the latter), and a special interest in maintaining an attractive home. Those very domestic concerns which the female pioneers (viewing them as unwanted burdens) had so vigorously rejected, have today become desirable, and willingly assumed, activities.

Today one can scarcely enter an apartment before the food is brought out—cookies, a cake, or a pie, and sometimes two kinds of cake or two pies—all of which the hostess has prepared herself. This is made possible by the fact that today each apartment is furnished with a stove, and the kibbutz kitchen is available for flour, sugar, eggs, and so on—both innovations, needless to say, having been introduced upon the insistence of women. Moreover, adverting to the second domestic characteristic, the apartment one enters is almost unrecognizably different from the rooms remembered from 1951. The wooden boxes and cots of an earlier epoch had of course, been replaced by real furniture even at that time. But today, with each family being supplied with a cash allowance for furniture, the women have been able to make their own decisions concerning the decoration of the apartment, rather than accepting the standardized kibbutz furniture available in 1951. Today, therefore, individual styles and tastes are reflected, for example, in elegant furniture of Danish design. Indeed, the elegance of the furnishing in some of the apartments has led some old-timers to characterize sneeringly the drawing rooms of some of the younger sabras as "salons," or (what is even worse) as "just like Tel Aviv."

It is of interest to observe, in connection with this return to femininity, that in a recent study of "feminine" attitudes among Israeli women, as measured by their self-descriptions on a feminine attitude scale, kibbutz women were discovered to be more "feminine" than other Israeli women. (What is even more unexpected the women of Kibbutz Artzi were more "feminine" than those of other kibbutz federations.)[5] Specifically, as measured by the items on this scale, kibbutz women are more "tender," and more "submissive," show a greater preference for distinctively "feminine" occupations and hobbies, and more strongly reject specifically "masculine" tasks. These findings, not surprisingly, characterize the attitudes of the younger much more than the older generation, the latter exhibiting greater fidelity to the feminist ideology of the kibbutz.

In this chapter I have described a counterrevolution both in culture (ideology) and social structure. Culturally, this counterrevolution, which perhaps can best be characterized as a return from radical feminism to femininity, has been marked by two important features. First, the repudiation of the view that the psychological and behavioral differences between the sexes are cultural in favor of the view that at least many of these differences are natural. Second, the repudiation of the "identity" meaning of sexual equality in favor of its "equivalence" meaning. Structurally, this counterrevolution can be described as a return to sex-role differentiation in the economic system and to a more traditional emphasis on the importance of marriage and family roles, following earlier efforts to abolish the former system and to reconstitute the latter roles.

Each aspect of this counterrevolution—the cultural and the structural—raises a vital question. The first question is explanatory: how are we to account for the return of the female sabras to a preference for "female" over "male" occupations and for their reassignment of family roles to a position of affective centrality? Assuming that the determinants of these changes can be identified, their panhuman implications are obvious: do the "feminine" orientations of the sabras reflect generic female characteristics, or are they the consequences of historical determinants specific to the kibbutz? The second question is evaluative: has the reemergence of sex-role differentiation in the kibbutz economy and of more traditional forms of

5. This study, conducted by the Department of Psychology of the University of Tel Aviv, was reported in the Israeli weekly, *Chotam*, July 11, 1975 (in Hebrew).

marriage and the family signalled a return to sexual inequality, as some observers (both inside and outside the kibbutz movement) have contended? Here too, the panhuman implications are obvious: does the condition of sexual equality require that males and females occupy structurally identical statuses (the "identity" meaning of equality), or is it sufficient that their statuses, however different, be of equal value (the "equivalence" meaning of equality)? I shall deal with the second question in the next chapter, deferring the first to the following chapter.

# Chapter 3. The reality of sexual equality

Although many social scientists believe that the sabra counterrevolution has resulted in a falling away from both the ideal and practice of sexual equality in the kibbutz, this conclusion requires careful scrutiny before it can be accepted. In such a scrutiny the first task, obviously, is to establish a set of criteria by which this conclusion, or any other, might be assessed. Blumberg (1974), in a recent cross-cultural study of the status of women, has offered such a set. From a structural point of view, at least, the status of women, she has suggested, can be measured by the power of women, relative to men, to influence the outcome of a set of "life options" which confront both sexes in any society. Since these life options relate primarily, though not exclusively, to events associated with marriage and the family, they provide an excellent set of criteria for assessing sexual equality within the domestic domain. They include the following (Blumberg 1974:5): (1) whether and whom to marry, (2) termination of marriage, (3) pre- and extramarital sex, (4) determination of family size (including interventions to restrict its size), (5) freedom of movement, (6) access to education, and (7) household authority.

With respect to these criteria, surely, kibbutz women may be said to be fully equal to men. Thus, (1) males and females alike have complete freedom in regard to marriage, (2) this also holds for divorce, (3) both may engage with impunity in premarital sex, while extramarital sex (though it occurs) is disapproved for both, (4) decisions concerning family size, as well as the techniques employed for its control, are made jointly, (5) women enjoy the same freedom of movement, both within and outside the kibbutz, as men, (6) women not only have equal access to education but also more women receive higher education than men, (7) household authority (in regard to children, allocation of economic resources, and the like) is shared by both.

Since all this is obvious to even a casual observer of the kibbutz movement, we can only conclude that those social scientists who view the sabra counterrevolution as a falling away from sexual equality are referring to changes outside of the domestic domain. Blumberg herself (1974:6, 7) characterizes these changes as an "erosion" of and a "retreat" from sexual equality in the kibbutz; and Kanter (1976:662) contends that these changes indicate that the kibbutz has not only failed to create "equality and equity between the sexes," but that it "departs" from the ideal of equality. Similarly, the Israeli sociologist Padan-Eisenstark (1975:502), argues that because "there is a clear distinction between 'female' and 'male' occupations," there is no sexual equality in the kibbutz. An Israeli journalist, commenting on the increasing familism of kibbutz women, is even more insistent on this point. "Equality," she writes, "is exactly what the modern kibbutz woman does not want. Although she lives in an environment designed in large part to 'free the woman from the yoke of domestic service,' as the old kibbutz slogan put it, the young kibbutz woman of today is determinedly setting about to change her environment so that she can again bear that yoke, this time of her own free will" (Hazelton 1977:131). Even Leviatan, a kibbutz member as well as a social scientist, argues that the fact that kibbutz women today place family above work (whereas men reverse the priority) "proves that efforts for the equalization of the sexes were unsuccessful" (Leviatan 1975:23).

Although the consensus of these diverse observers cannot be lightly dismissed, it is nevertheless my judgment that the sabra counterrevolution has not resulted in a diminution in sexual equality as a kibbutz ideal and that the status of kibbutz women indicates that this ideal has been substantially (though not entirely) achieved. This judgment, moreover, applies not only to the domestic domain (marriage and the family), but to the economic domain (the sexual division of labor) as well. In order to examine the grounds for this judgment, we must again establish a set of criteria for the assessment of equality in the latter domain.

If, by definition, equality is construed in its "identity" meaning (see supra, p. 7), then of course any form of sex-role differentiation is itself proof of sexual inequality in practice; and the sabra view that such differentiation is a natural state of affairs is proof that sexual equality is no longer even a kibbutz ideal. It is in accordance with this meaning of equality that the social scientists quoted above argue that sexual equality is no longer found in the kibbutz. The notion, however, that diversity necessarily entails inequality is hardly a self-evident truth. As Alice Rossi has observed, "where age and sex are concerned, diversity is a biological fact, while equality is a political, ethical, and social precept. Marxist theory notwithstanding, there is no rule of nature or social organization that says men and women have to be the same or do the same things in order to be socially, economically, and politically equal" (Rossi 1977:2). In short, if sexual equality is taken in its "equivalence" meaning (see supra, p. 8), sex-role differentiation is not, a priori, a sufficient condition for sexual inequality; and the question of whether sexual specialization in the kibbutz economy can be said to be characterized by sexual inequality then becomes an empirical question.

If we adopt the "equivalence" meaning of equality, there are (or so at least it seems to me) five criteria for assessing the degree to which any system of economic specialization, whether based on sex or on any other attribute, may be said to be characterized by inequality. First, for any category of social actors, is recruitment to the various specialties based on systematically discriminatory qualifications? Second, even if it is not discriminatory, does the recruitment system result in the allocation of any category of social actors to (culturally defined) low-status occupations? Third, for any category of social actors does the allocation result in a discriminatory or inequitable reward structure? Fourth, for any category of social actors, does the allocation result in discriminatory or inequitable working conditions? Fifth, regardless of the assessment of outside observers, does any category of social actors perceive the system (by any of the above criteria) to be discriminatory? Using these criteria let us now examine the sexual division of labor found in the kibbutz.

To begin with the first criterion, the reemergence of sexual specialization in the early days of the kibbutz, by which women became increasingly concentrated in educational and service branches, was based neither on cultural (prejudice) nor structural (discrimination) barriers to the recruitment of women to so-called "male" (or any other) occupations. Rather, as we observed in a previous chapter, it was based primarily on an interaction of two other variables: (a) the biological disadvantage of women in agricultural occupations, and (b) a commitment (on the part of both sexes) to rising levels of investment and consumption. This is not to deny that in some cases at least it was also based on sex-role typing. That this, however, is a sufficient sign of prejudice or discrimination cannot be judged by current polemical struggles. For, despite these polemics, the degree to which some sex-role typing might accurately reflect true sexual differences, rather than hidden (and not so hidden) prejudice, remains scientifically moot.

Moot or not, the sex-role typing in the kibbutz was shared, it will be recalled, by men and women alike, rather than imposed by men on the women. This does not mean, as I shall have occasion to observe below, that true sexual prejudice (in contrast to sex-role typing) was absent from the kibbutz in its early years, or has disappeared from the kibbutz today. Since, however, this prejudice was and is individual and isolated, rather than institutionalized, it did not have a major impact either on the origins of the sexual division of labor in the kibbutz or (what is more germane) on the contemporary recruitment of women to their economic roles. That the system was not, and is not, based on systematically discriminatory recruitment practices is, I think, indisputable. In short, by the first criterion (discriminatory recruitment), there is little evidence that the sexual division of labor in the kibbutz is based on sexual inequality.

Turning to the second criterion (the economic reward structure), it can be stated categorically that sexual differentiation in the economic role system has never been associated with sexual differentiation in the economic reward system. Indeed, rather than merely receiving the same pay for the same type of work (equity), men and women receive the same pay regardless of their type of work (equality). In the kibbutz, of course, "pay" refers to goods and services rather than a cash salary; and however different their occupations may be, and whatever differences there might exist in their economic importance, men and women receive goods and services of equal or equivalent economic value.

This radical sexual equality in economic reward is entailed, of course, by the general principle of equality that informs the kibbutz economy. Nevertheless, in assessing the degree to which sexual equality is found in the kibbutz, we cannot ignore the fact that, in its application, this principle applies without qualification to sex as well. Hence, the general manager of the kibbutz economy, a male, receives the same pay as a female who, for example, works in the kitchen. In sum, by the second criterion (reward structure) sex-role differentiation in the economy has not produced sexual inequality.

If we now turn to the third criterion (status structure), the situation is much more ambiguous. By the present division of labor, women are concentrated in services and education, which are less prestigeful than the farming branches, which are preponderantly male specialties. Moreover, the invidious distinction between "nonproductive" (education and services) and "productive" (farming and industrial) labor in itself suggests that by this third criterion the division of labor in the kibbutz is characterized by sexual inequality. Nevertheless, this conclusion is not entirely valid. Although women are concentrated in education and services, some work in kibbutz industry as well as in such farming branches as the dairy and poultry run. Moreover, many service occupations are male specialties, and to the extent that services enjoy lower status than agriculture, this holds for the men's specialties as much as the women's. Thus, whether it be carpentry, newspaper editing, electricity, and construction (to cite some male occupations), or teaching, child care, cooking, and nursing (to cite some female occupations), all are less prestigeful than, for example, wheat or cotton production. This being the case, it cannot be concluded that the kibbutz division of labor has produced a sexually stratified status system, one in which male occupations enjoy higher status than female occupations. Rather, it is a system in which one category of preponderantly male occupations enjoys higher status than all other occupations, both male and female.

Nevertheless, since most females in this occupational status system have a lower status occupation than some males, it can be said that by the criterion we are considering (status equality) the sexual division of labor is characterized to a certain extent by sexual inequality. This inequality in practice, however, hardly signals a retreat from the ideal of sexual equality. Agricultural occupations occupy the top of the economic status hierarchy, not because they are male specialties, but, as we have seen, because of historical reasons entirely unrelated to sexual status. First, the regnant value of agriculture was a basic tenet of the socialist-Zionist ideology that led to the founding of the kibbutz movement. This ideology was adopted by the pioneer men and women at the same time that they formulated the ideal of sexual equality, and long before agriculture became a male specialty. At that time they saw no incompatibility between the moral primacy of agriculture and the ideal of sexual equality since they assumed that men and women were equally qualified for agricultural labor. It was because this assumption proved to be untenable that women withdrew from agriculture; and since the feminist ideology of the women impelled them to express their emancipation in farm labor, they, no less than the men, forced the distinction between high status farming and low status service occupations. Second, as the demands on the kibbutz economy (for both investment and consumption) led to increasing needs for capital, agricultural labor acquired even more status because of the distinction that developed between the "productive," or income-producing farming occupations, and the "nonproductive," or income-consuming service occupations. And since farming had already become a male specialty, men just happened to become the beneficiaries of this status distinction.

In short, although status inequality may characterize to some extent the sexual division of labor in the kibbutz in practice, it does not represent a retreat from sexual equality as an ideal. Rather, it represents the unanticipated consequence of a simultaneous commitment to incompatible values. Since, however, the ideology associated with agricultural labor is becoming progressively attenuated, and since the growing prosperity of the kibbutz is producing a weakening of the traditional distinction between productive and nonproductive labor, there are some grounds for believing that the status of the sexes will, in practice, increasingly approximate the ideal of sexual equality which has remained a strong kibbutz ideal.

It must be added, however, that accompanying the development of the status differentiation between income-producing and income-consuming branches, there also developed a differentiation in the allocation of resources to those branches. To maximize their productive capacities, the working conditions in the farming branches (as well as such service branches as the machine shop and the electrical shop that contribute to the efficiency of the productive branches) have consistently been better than those in services and education. From the very beginning the latter branches have been the last to receive modern equipment or improved working conditions. As a male sabra in Kiryat Yedidim—and an ardent feminist—recently put it: "Today every man in agriculture works with a machine that is worth at least 100,000 [Israeli] pounds, while the women in the kitchen still scrub floors with the same old rags." Although this may be somewhat exaggerated, the general thrust of his argument is sound. It was only recently, for example, that Kiryat Yedidim installed air conditioners in the children's houses, sewing room, or ironing room—although the heat of the Israeli summer can be oppressive indeed—and even today there is still no air conditioning in the kitchen.

Although these examples are taken from Kiryat Yedidim, the problem (as all the conferences dealing with the status of kibbutz women indicate) is found in all kibbutzim. As assessed, then, by the fourth criterion (equality in working conditions), it can be concluded that the sexual division of labor is, de facto, characterized by sexual inequality. Again, however, there is little evidence that this is symptomatic of a retreat from the ideal of sexual equality. It is significant, for example, that the women themselves, though not at all reluctant to complain about the lagging improvement in the working conditions in their branches, have done little to effect more rapid improvement in these conditions. That they have not done so—and since the kibbutz is a participatory democracy par excellence, they could easily have affected the necessary changes by their votes at the general assembly—indicates their recognition that sexual discrimination is not the issue. Rather, the issue, which they approve in principle while complaining of its consequences, is economic prosperity. To achieve economic growth and to maintain its competitive position, the kibbutz must continuously improve the efficiency of its productive branches, which means that the service branches and education cannot have an equal claim on the scarce resources of the economy. That this principle, shared by men and women alike (because, of course, they both benefit from it), leads to sexual inequality in working conditions cannot be denied, but this is an adventitious consequence of the sexual distribution of the labor force, and not an indifference to, let alone a retreat from, the ideal of sexual equality. Indeed, despite the differential lag in working conditions, the service branches have undergone dramatic improvements in the past quarter century; and in many kibbutzim the service areas, including the kitchen, which had always been the prototype of this problem (Spiro 1955:227), have become models of good working conditions.

To conclude, assessed on the basis of the fourth criterion (working conditions), the sexual division of labor in the kibbutz has resulted to some degree (and sometimes to a large degree) in sexual inequality in practice, but it has not produced a retreat from the ideal of sexual equality.

Let us now turn to the subjective criterion for the assessment of sexual inequality: to what degree do the women themselves view the kibbutz system of sex-role differentiation as unequal? To deal properly with this last criterion, we must distinguish their early views from their later ones. The view of the early pioneers was unambiguous. For them, subscribing as they did to the "identity" meaning of sexual equality, sex-role differentiation, as such, was ipso facto a mark of status inequality (our third criterion). Hence the reemergence of sexual specialization in the economy was not only viewed by them as de facto inequality, but it also signaled a serious departure from the ideal of equality. Moreover, the particular form which the system took in the kibbutz exacerbated their view of its inequality. Since these women themselves had viewed farming as the occupation of the highest status—and women's equal participation in farming as the ultimate mark of female emancipation—the gradual concentration of women in nonfarming occupations was for them a most invidious form of inequality. That men, too, worked in nonfarming occupations did not allay their feelings because, of course, it was they (the women) and not the men who had the need to prove their worth. Since, moreover, they had viewed the biological differentiation of the sexes as irrelevant to their role differentiation, the fact that the women's biological disadvantage for farming was the basic cause of the sexual division of labor made their frustration all the more acute: it meant, of course, that the ideal of sexual equality, as they construed it, could never be achieved.

Today, turning to the current scene, these views are all but dead. If very few female sabras work in farming, it is not because these branches are closed to them, but because (as we have seen) they have no wish to enter them. They do not find them intrinsically desirable, and, having rejected the "identity" meaning of sexual equality, they have no special need to perform "men's" work as a means to or as a necessary symbol of sexual equality. Indeed, since they do not view sex-role differentiation, as such, as a mark of sexual inequality, they do not take it as a sign of inferiority that farming is a male specialty. On the contrary, many of them, viewing sexual specialization as "natural," say that it is not natural for women to wish to work in agriculture. Consider, for example, the following statement made by a young sabra woman at an interkibbutz conference on sexual equality: "What is the importance of sexual equality [in its "identity" meaning]? As one born in the kibbutz, I never

once felt the need for this kind of sexual equality. The sex-role differentiation in work and in administrative posts strikes me as natural,
and entirely nondiscriminatory. Why is it [identity of the sexes]
necessary? Is it really necessary for a pregnant woman to drive a
tank?" Another young sabra, a twenty-three year old college student,
when asked if there was sexual equality in the kibbutz [in its "identity" meaning] put it this way: "Yes I think there is, so far as opportunity is concerned, but so far as desire is concerned, no. That is,
women do not aspire to equality [in its "identity" meaning], but if
they aspired to it, they could achieve it."

The attitudes of female sabras are echoed by males, as the following statement by a forty-year-old personnel manager of a kibbutz
factory indicates: "There is no sexual equality [in its "identity" mean-
ing] in the kibbutz; there is no need for it. That is just mechanical
equality. Why should we think that child care should be assigned to
men, and that women should be assigned elsewhere? Women cannot
do many of the things that men are adapted to do because the physical capacities of a man permit him to perform certain tasks better
than women. On the other hand, with respect to early child care, I
don't think men are as qualified as women."

Given these attitudes it is not surprising that the great majority
of the sabras in our six-kibbutz survey of both males and females
agreed that sexual equality remains a primary characteristic of the
kibbutz, not only as an ideal, but also in practice. Only 14 percent of
each sex disagreed with this generalization.

We may now summarize our findings. Although sexual equality,
in its "identity" meaning, is no longer found in the kibbutz economy,
either in practice or as an ideal, this generalization does not hold for
the "equivalence" meaning of equality. Since the latter meaning is the
one to which the sabras subscribe, and since by this meaning the sexual division of labor in the kibbutz economy is marked by only a mod-
erate degree of inequality which, moreover, did not result from (or
lead to) a diminution in the ideal of equality, and since finally the
social actors do not view it as unequal, it would seem not unwarranted to conclude that the reemergence of sex-role differentiation
in the kibbutz economy has not lead to an "erosion" of sexual equality
in the economic domain.

But equality, after all, is only one dimension of work satisfaction,
and the fact that the sexual division of labor in the kibbutz is not

characterized by any marked degree of sexual inequality, does not mean that kibbutz women find satisfaction in their work. The fact is that for many women the "problem of the woman" (*ba-yat ha-chavera*) is as acute today as it was in 1951 (cf. Spiro 1955:201 ff), and one of the most important factors contributing to this problem is work discontent. For although most women approve of sex-role differentiation and have no desire to work in male specialties, many of them also evince little desire to work in the female specialties available to them in the kibbutz. The reason is not difficult to discern.

Since a kibbutz is a small village—the adult population ranges from 100 to 1000, 200 being average—its range of occupations is very narrow, and since contemporary kibbutz women have little interest in agriculture or the trades (carpentry, construction, and the like), the effective range of occupations available to women is even more restricted. With some few exceptions, their alternatives are confined to the laundry, kitchen, clothing room, children's house, and school. Many women are quite content with these alternatives and find much satisfaction in their work, but many others are frustrated and bitter because the system compels them to choose an occupation for which they have neither talent nor interest. Even those who have the opportunity to study or train in a field of their own interest (and the kibbutzim have been increasingly supportive of the needs and desires of such women) generally end up working in one of the former occupations, usually early child care. In Kiryat Yedidim, for example, one young sabra with a college degree in chemistry is now working in the nursery school. Although the kibbutz was willing to finance her scientific education, it was unable to provide her with a suitable job: there simply are no occupational outlets for a chemist (male or female) in the kibbutz. Another young sabra, with a degree in fine arts, works as a bookkeeper in the business office, because the school system cannot absorb another art teacher. It should not be surprising, then, that 93 percent of the women in our six-kibbutz sample maintained that women are not happy in their work because of the limited range of occupations available to them. It is important to note that the men agreed with this judgment, and by an equally large majority.

Since, with the increase in the kibbutz birth rate, the largest single group of women now work in early child care, it is among them in particular that complaints about the paucity of vocational alternatives are most frequently heard. In addition to their lack of interest in this work, for which many claim to be temperamentally unsuited, there are yet other reasons for their discontent. The hours are long, the responsibility great, and the tensions (generated especially by the more anxious mothers) high. Moreover, child-care workers must be on duty both on weekdays and certain Saturdays, and during the day as well as in the evening, which means that they have less time to devote to their own children. To cap their discontent, in order to qualify for work that they dislike, they must undergo a long period of formal education—as much as three years for nursery teachers—in which many have little interest. The ultimate irony of this situation was epitomized by the comment of a young sabra of my acquaintance who, unhappy with her work in child care, was granted a leave to take a year's refresher course: "Thank goodness, I can get away from the children for a whole year."

If, because it employs the largest group of women, child care accounts for a high percentage of the women's occupational discontent, other female specialties also evoke their proportionate share of dissatisfaction—not so much, however, because the women claim to be temperamentally unsuited for the work, nor again because it is especially hard, but because it is "boring." For kibbutz women, who are among the best educated women in Israel, to spend their entire workday in the laundry, the sewing room, and the like, is—in a word—boring. In this respect the situation today is no different from what I found in 1951. I pointed then (Spiro 1955:229) to the paradox that although the kibbutz innovations in marriage and the family (including collective socialization) achieved their aims of liberating the women from the domestic domain, they had not freed them from domestic labor. Given the sexual division of labor in the kibbutz, today (as in 1951) most women in the kibbutz (like most women elsewhere) care for children, prepare meals, launder clothes, and so on. Nevertheless, there is a difference in this regard between kibbutz and nonkibbutz women, and the difference, ironically enough, is to the disadvantage of kibbutz women. Whereas other women cook *and* sew *and* launder *and* care for children, kibbutz women cook *or* sew *or* launder *or* care for children. The latter regimen, to be sure, is much easier, but it is also much less stimulating, and for educated women it can be downright boring.

In sum, if kibbutz women are unhappy in their work roles, it is not because the sexual division of labor either frustrates their desire to enter male occupations or produces sexual inequality, but because the kibbutz, as a small village, cannot offer them the wide range of female occupations which they could find in a large city. Some of the latter occupations for which they have expressed an interest are simply not available to them in a kibbutz because they are not required (retail selling, for example), or they are not in demand (law, for example), or they are in oversupply (nursing, for example). Not surprisingly, therefore, although 40 percent of the young women in Kibbutz Artzi between the ages of 23 and 25 (those who have recently returned from army service) said they were discontented with their present occupation, most of them were unable to state a greater preference for any of the other occupations available to women in the kibbutz (Menachem Rosner, in Anonymous 1974:22).

For the sabra women, then, who (contrary to the early feminist ideology of the kibbutz) have rejected the "identity" meaning of sexual equality in favor of its "equivalence" meaning, women's liberation consists not in the freedom to perform the male occupation of kibbutz men, but in the opportunity to perform the female (and sexually undifferentiated) occupations available to nonkibbutz women. And in the long run their restricted opportunity poses a much graver problem for the future of the kibbutz than the earlier problem of sexual inequality (if there were such a problem) could ever have posed. With effort and good will, the problem of sexual inequality can be solved (as experience has demonstrated) by and in the kibbutz. But short of highly imaginative and extensive planning, the problem of expanded opportunity can find a solution only outside the kibbutz, and unless such planning is undertaken, many women may increasingly seek just such a solution.

That the kibbutz has not been entirely successful in solving the economic "problem of the woman" is, then, rather evident. But it is surely misguided to contend that this "problem" was created by the emergence of sex-role differentiation or that the essence of the problem consists in either the lack of, or a retreat fom the ideal of, sexual equality. Rather, the emergence of sex-role differentiation represented a recognition on the part of men and women alike that there are important physical and psychological differences between the sexes, and that the occupational distribution of the sexes must take these differences into account. That the limitation of roles available to them has led to discontent on the part of many kibbutz women is a function of the demographic (small population), ecological (rural settlement), and economic (agriculturally based) characteristics of the kibbutz, rather than of sexual inequality. That these same characteristics may produce work discontent among kibbutz men, as well, indicates that sexual equality is not the issue. Thus, men who are interested in careers in science, journalism, the arts, and so on, face the same problem as the women whose career interests cannot be satisfied in a community with these characteristics. Since, however, this book is about women, we need not enter into this "problem of the man." I should merely note in passing that this issue, as it effects men and women alike, is one with which the kibbutz movement is struggling to find a solution.

What, then, about sexual equality in the political domain? The same critics who view sex-role differentiation in the kibbutz economy as a mark of sexual inequality, maintain that the unequal distribution of the sexes in kibbutz governance is yet another indication of sexual inequality in the kibbutz: men, so it is claimed, hold power, and women are subordinate to them. Anyone acquainted with the kibbutz recognizes, however, that of all the charges concerning sexual inequality, this is the least defensible. All major policy decisions in the kibbutz are recommended by the secretariat (*mazkirut*), and decided upon by the general assembly (the entire kibbutz membership). The secretariat comprises the following elected officials: economic manager (who is always a male), the secretary (who may be either a male or a female or—in those kibbutzim in which there are two secretaries—a male and a female), and the chairmen of certain key committees (who may be either male or female). To be sure, since many women are uninterested in elective office, there are typically fewer women than men in the secretariat, but this tells us more about kibbutz women than about sexual equality.

I have already observed, however, that men have only slightly more interest than women in elective office. There are a number of reasons for this, not the least of which being the disproportionate ratio of rights to duties, and the relative lack of power, inherent in these offices, as well as the great amount of time which they require and which most kibbutz members would rather devote to other activities. As a result most candidates for office agree to serve only after considerable (and often unpleasant) haggling with the nominating committees or with the general assembly. Depending upon one's view of the role and function of power in human affairs, this situation may or may not be characterized as a bad feature of the kibbutz social system, but the making of such a normative judgment is not my present concern. I stress this point rather in order to indicate that kibbutz women have not been subordinated to men who, desirous of and having achieved political power, have relegated the women to an inferior and dependent political status.

It is true, of course, that policies concerning the allocation of economic resources in the kibbutz are recommended to the secretariat, and ultimately to the general assembly, by the economic committee, and that the latter (headed by the economic manager) is comprised primarily (and sometimes exclusively) of men. It is also true that the general assembly, often unacquainted with (or bored by) the intricate recommendations of the economic committee, usually ratifies them without much debate. That this reflects, however, a condition of sexual inequality—unless, of course, any type of sex-role differentiation is viewed, a priori, as unequal—is equally hard to defend. Women typically do not serve on the economic committee for the same reason that they do not serve as economic manager: since, by their own desires, few women work in the agricultural and industrial branches of the kibbutz economy, they typically have neither the experience nor the interest to deal with these matters. Perhaps they ought to have such experience or such interest, but again this is a normative judgment which has no place in the present discussion.

On a nonnormative level, however, it can be easily demonstrated that their lack of participation in the deliberations of the economic committee does not relegate kibbutz women to a position of economic subordination to men. Women prepare the budgets for those economic branches which they head or in which they are active, and in the debates and votes concerning the overall kibbutz budget, they have exactly the same rights as men. That they have successfully exercised these rights is demonstrated by the fact that the major changes in consumption policies that have taken place over the years (which need not be discussed here) have been primarily at the initiative of the women.

From this evaluation of the status and roles of women in the domestic, economic, and political domains, we may conclude that, despite the sabra counterrevolution in marriage, the family, and sex-role differentiation, the kibbutz has not fallen away from either the ideal or the practice of sexual equality. This same judgment holds for the overall social status of the sexes, as evaluated by the attitudes and perceptions of the adult sabras. Thus, interviews with the sabras in our six-kibbutz sample indicate that they view males and females as completely equal in intelligence, in intellectual capacity, in their worth as human beings, and in their contributions to kibbutz society. They hold that sexual differences in social roles, including leadership roles, reflect differences in interests and needs rather than in talent or ability. Moreover, these attitudes and perceptions are reflected in their judgments and assessments of each other as individuals. In Kiryat Yedidim, the kibbutz I know best, it is quite clear that those individuals who occupy the highest rung of the prestige and respect hierarchies comprise males and females in more or less equal proportion. In short, it is not only as members of a social category, but also as individuals that females enjoy equality with males in the kibbutz.

Having attempted to answer the first major question raised by the counterrevolution in the kibbutz—the question of sexual equality—we may now turn to the second: what are the possible determinants of this counterrevolution?

# Chapter 4. The determinants of the counter-revolution

## Introduction

That the counterrevolutionary transformations described in the previous chapters are a function of some basic parameters of human existence (social, psychological, and biological) is supported by the fact that this process has occurred not in a few kibbutzim, but in the entire kibbutz movement. Indeed, it is precisely because of its uniformity that the problem of disentangling its determinants is a formidable (and perhaps an ultimately impossible) task; for, of course, in the absence of variability the inquiry must proceed without any built-in (let alone experimental) controls. This is bad enough in any inquiry, but the difficulty is compounded in this case because evidence can be marshalled to plausibly support the claims of both polar types of determinism—biological and cultural; and inasmuch as the polemical context in which contemporary discussions of women are embedded arouses strong affect, a dispassionate assessment of either type is difficult to achieve.

Let us take, for example, the emergence of a system of sexual specialization in the kibbutz economy in the early history of the kibbutz movement, even prior to the entrance of the sabras into the economy. As observed in a previous chapter, this change was produced by the interaction of three variables: (a) a subsistence economy and an ideology for which farm labor was an adaptive requirement and a regnant value, respectively, (b) the biological disadvantage of women in physically demanding occupations, (c) the kibbutz commitment to rising levels of investment and consumption. Notice then, that if the subsistence economy had been based, for example, on business or basketmaking, rather than farming, the biological differentiation of the sexes would have had no consequences for their economic differentiation. Similarly, if the pioneers had not been committed to the ideology of socialist-Zionism, then, despite its pragmatic importance, farming would not have become an ultimate value, and the differentiation of farming from nonfarming labor would not have entailed a status differentiation of males and females. Moreover, even with the emphasis (pragmatic or ideological) on farming, if the pioneers (males and females alike) had been willing to sustain a lower standard of living or a lower rate of economic growth, the relative physical inefficiency of women would not have compelled them to retire from farm labor, and men as well as women could have been assigned to those service branches which have become female specialties. Again, if the pioneers had had little or no desire for children, women would not have been deterred from working in those agricultural branches which, allegedly, contributed to miscarriage. Further, if an alternative had been considered for breast feeding, women could have remained in their physically distant farm jobs, rather than transferring to service occupations which were in closer proximity to the infants' house. Finally, despite the increasing birth rate, males as well as females could have been assigned to work in the educational system if, again, productive efficiency had not been a primary economic concern, or if alternatively—for the data on this point are ambiguous —the founders (males and females alike) had not viewed early child care as a "natural" female specialty.

Most of these "ifs," however, yield ambiguous interpretations. Thus, if (as some would argue) the concern for rising levels of consumption and investment is a uniquely Western value, or if the desire for children and the stress on breast feeding are motivated by culturally acquired needs, then the reemergence of sex-role differentiation is best interpreted as a cultural artifact. That it reemerged so early, even in a social system that aimed to abolish it, might then be taken as supporting the thesis that fundamental change in sex roles requires massive, or draconian measures, of a degree and kind that the kibbutz pioneers were unable or unwilling to undertake. If, on the other hand, these particular values and motives are the expressions (as others would argue) of underlying human social and psychological orientations, the fact that a sexual division of labor was established by the very pioneers who were determined to destroy it, might then be taken as evidence for the thesis that sex-role differentiation is an institutional consequence of basic human motives and sentiments.

Clearly, then, any assessment of the determinants of the counter-revolution, insofar as the pioneers themselves were its agents, will inevitably be influenced by our antecedently held theories concerning the relative influence of external ("culture") versus internal ("na-ture") variables on human affairs. For those theorists for whom the organism is an "empty box" at birth, the assessment of these determinants will be slanted in the former direction. For those for whom the organism is "wired" in certain ways from birth, or for whom the characteristics of human social systems, whatever their differences, produce a set of invariant psychological dispositions in their developing infants, the assessment will be slanted in the latter direction. Thus, for example, the latter theorists could argue that the counterrevolution of the pioneer women was an expression of uni-versal female dispositions ("nature") which had been suppressed as part of their adolescent rebellion against the values of their parents. As they became older, however, and their rebellion had run its natural course, these dispositions were once again able to assert themselves. The "empty-box" theorists could just as plausibly argue, however, that the counterrevolution of the pioneers was not an expression of sup-pressed female dispositions, but a regression to values ("culture") which the women had acquired in the process of early socialization. For although they (together with the men) had initiated a feminist revolution, inasmuch as they were products of a traditional cultural and social system, they had to undo traditional values with which they had been imbued from infancy. Since, however, the influence of early learning (as any student of child development and every psy-chotherapist knows) is not easily overcome, their counterrevolution can be interpreted as a return to deeply engrained traditional values.

Since, then, there seems to be no way of resolving the conflict be-tween nativistic and acquired theories of the counterrevolution of the pioneer women, I intend to take a different tack: instead of dealing with the pioneers, I shall restrict the scope of our inquiry to the sabra women for whom it is somewhat easier to disentangle the relative contributions of "nature" and "culture." Thus, for example, since the sabras were reared in a feminist learning environment, we can cer-tainly rule out the hypothesis that their participation in the counter-revolution represents a return to deeply engrained values. In their case, on the contrary, the counterrevolution has taken place not be-cause of the reassertion of feminine values inculcated in childhood, but in spite of—indeed, in opposition to—the feminist values in which they had been trained. Hence, although the empirical task of discovering the determinants of the counterrevolution may be just as difficult for the sabras as for the pioneers, the logical strategy required to accomplish this task is much clearer.

This strategy requires in the first place that we identify all of the empirically plausible determinants of the counterrevolution which, in effect, means that we must distinguish the various determinants of human social behavior. In this connection we may distinguish, as ideal types, six sets of such determinants. (1) One set consists of variables "external" to the actors in respect to which their behavior is a more or less adaptive response. Within this set we may distinguish two subsets. (1a) One subset consists of those features of the physical environment to which social and cultural behavior may be viewed as adaptive responses. These "ecological" determinants, as we may call them, need not be considered here for both the revolution of the pioneers and the counterrevolution of the sabras have occurred in the same ecological setting. (And, it might be added, Bedouin encampments had often previously existed in the same ecological conditions.) This is not to deny the importance of ecology; it is merely to say that the adaptive requirements posed by ecological conditions can be satisfied in a variety of ways. (1b) A second subset of external determinants consists of variables comprising the human environment (social, economic, political, cultural) which, whatever the motivational dispositions of the actors, stimulate some kind of adaptive reaction. I shall designate this subset of external variables as "sociocultural" determinants.

(2) A second set of determinants consists of variables "internal" to the actors (desires, needs, wishes) which, as motivational dispositions, actively instigate their behavior. Within this set, however, we may distinguish four subsets. (2a) One subset is produced by cultural values and norms which are acquired by the actors in the enculturation process. Although initially "external" to the actors, inasmuch as these values and norms are "internalized" by them, they are transformed into needs, wishes, and the like which constitute internal instigations to behavior. I shall denote these motivational dispositions as "psychocultural" determinants. To the extent that many cultural norms and values are culturally variable, many of these motivational dispositions may be expected to vary from society to society. (2b) A

second subset of internal determinants comprise those needs and wishes which are acquired by children, prior to their acquisition of cultural values, from early social experiences. To the extent that certain—but by no means all—patterns of early child care represent institutional solutions to adaptive requirements of human beings as a biological species, these experiences are based on characteristics of human society which are more or less invariant. Hence, these motivational dispositions, unlike the former type, may be expected to be panhuman in their distribution.. Since, then, these needs and wishes, though precultural, are nevertheless social in their origin, I shall denote them as "psychosocial" determinants. (2c) A third subset of internal determinants consists of those needs and wishes which are acquired from experiences based on invariant characteristics of the human organism rather than of society. Since these needs are acquired as a result of the actors' experience of their bodies, I shall denote these motivational dispositions as "psychobiological" determinants. They, too, of course are panhuman in their distribution. (2d) A fourth subset of internal determinants consists of biologically inherited species drives. Phylogenetically determined, these motivational dispositions, which may be denoted as "biological" determinants, are also panhuman in their distribution.

In summary, this typology identifies five types of possible determinants of the counterrevolution, of which two (1b and 2a) are cultural, two (2b and 2c) are precultural but social, and one (2d) is precultural because biological, in origin. With this typology in mind, we may now attempt to assess the empirical relevance of these alternative determinants.

## Adaptation to sociocultural determinants external to the actors

On the basis of the data presented in the previous chapters we may identify a number of external social and cultural variables which may plausibly have served as determinants of the sabra counterrevolution. First, we might point to the persistence of some traditional sexist values in kibbutz males. Although the male pioneers were intellectually committed to female liberation, it might be argued that they were not sufficiently emancipated from their European sexist attitudes to provide the male support required for the feminist revolution to succeed. Hence, despite the egalitarian ideology of the kibbutz, social relations between the sexes retained many aspects of their prerevolutionary relations, and in the resultant conflict between culture and social structure, the sabras, it might be argued, were more strongly influenced by the latter than the former. One can point to at least two kinds of evidence for this thesis.

In the first place, if the men had been sufficiently liberated, then, despite its adverse economic consequences, they would have been willing to share the traditionally defined "women's work"—child care, cooking, and so on—which would have precluded their becoming female specialties. Their refusal to do so not only contributed to the early establishment of sex-role differentiation in the kibbutz, but, it might be argued, it also laid the groundwork for the counterrevolutionary changes in the sabras, for insofar as the women were unable to achieve sexual equality in its "identity" meaning, they retreated to their roles as mothers and wives as a compensatory mechanism. In the second place, some few kibbutz males, both early and late, have expressed sexist attitudes which, though confined to a small minority, might nevertheless have encouraged the women's return to domestic roles. The following examples, all from Kibbutz Yedidim, are illustrative of such sexist attitudes. In 1951, a young sabra male, then in his twenties, said that sabra females were "worthless," that none evinced any "ability." In 1975, another sabra, also in his twenties, expressed almost identical attitudes when speaking of his female age peers: "All I want is that girls be attractive; in other respects they are not very talented." In 1951, a female sabra observed that if a woman spoke her mind at the general assembly, she was not listened to—for "the men know best." She said that men could "talk any kind of nonsense" at the general assembly, and there was no criticism, but if a woman were to speak in a similar vein, the men would laugh. If a woman expressed herself on the problem of education, "it's not worth anything," but if a man spoke on this subject, "it is wonderful." Again, a few years ago, after the general assembly had granted a leave of absence to a young woman to study art, a male pioneer who had opposed the decision angrily told her: "But don't think that because we have given you a year to *study* art, we will permit you to work as an artist. Art you can do in your spare time."

The invidious distinction between "productive" and "service" branches is plausibly a second external cultural determinant of the counterrevolution. Since the latter branches have always enjoyed less prestige in the kibbutz, many women did not achieve status equality in the economic domain even in the "equivalence" meaning of equality. This being the case, it might be argued, the female sabras turned to traditional marriage and family roles because in these roles their status was secure. This renewed emphasis on marriage and the family may also, it might be argued, have contributed to the sabras' renewed interest in feminine attractiveness. Having retreated from the economic marketplace as the appropriate avenue for status achievement they may then have turned to the enhancement of femininity as an alternative avenue.

A third plausible external determinant is the narrow range of economic roles available to the women. Since female occupations, as we have seen, are often monotonous, uninteresting, or difficult, sabra women may have turned to marriage and family roles in order to find other, noneconomic forms of creative and emotional satisfaction.

What, now, can we say about the importance of these three social and cultural variables in bringing about the sabra counterrevolution? Although it seems reasonable to assume that they had some influence on the changing attitudes of the sabras, it is doubtful, in my judgment, that they were the primary determinants. After all, a return to the status quo ante is not the only possible response to prejudice or discrimination; one need only point to the revolutionary stance of the pioneering generation to indicate that there are other alternatives. Moreover, if women reemphasized the importance of marriage and the family because of the lower prestige of "service," relative to "productive" branches, we would then want to ask why the large percentage of men who also work in services did not respond in the same way. Finally, although the range of economic roles occupied by women in the present sexual division of labor is very narrow, women are in no sense confined to "female" occupations. If, as I have already indicated, women today do not work in "male" occupations (including the "productive" agricultural branches), it is less because of social restrictions than because of their disinterest in them. Thus, despite their discontent with their work in services or child care, only a tiny minority of the women in our six-kibbutz sample expressed a wish to work in agriculture. When we directly asked them about this, the great majority rejected it as a desirable alternative.

In short, although it might be argued that the three social and cultural variables discussed above may account for the sabras' adaptation to the counterrevolutionary changes already instigated by the pioneers, it would be more difficult to argue that they also account for the fact that the sabras go much further than their pioneering mothers and grandmothers. The sabras, as we have seen, have not merely accepted the early counterrevolutionary changes, but they celebrate them; and, moreover, many of them wish to introduce still other changes of a more far-reaching character.

A fourth plausible external determinant of their counterrevolution is the system of child care in which the sabras were raised as children (which, in essentials, is the same as is found today). As children in 1951 it can be said that, on the one hand, they seemed always happy to return to the children's house after their daily visits with their parents. On the other hand, they were often distressed when their parents left them at night, and there is some evidence for the inference that they experienced this separation as rejection or abandonment. If the sabras felt deprived of proper parenting as children, then as adults (it might be argued) they may have developed a strong commitment to family roles from a desire to provide their own children with better parenting than they had received. The difficulty, however, with this interpretation is that it does not explain why the males, who presumably experienced the same childhood ambivalence, have not reacted in the same manner as the females.[1] Nor does it explain the female counterrevolution in sex-role differentiation.

In sum, from this discussion of the social and cultural conditions in the kibbutz, with respect to which the counterrevolution of the sabras may have been a reactive response, it is probably fair to conclude that their influence was not decisive. Hence, without wishing to

1. In fact, in a 1962 study of 17- and 18-year-old sabras (156 males and 158 females), more females than males reported (a) that, as children, they had wanted to spend more time with their parents, and (b) that when they become parents they will want to care for their own children more than their parents had cared for them (Rabin 1968). On the other hand, one of the intriguing findings of our six-kibbutz survey is that most of the sabras in our sample, including those who preferred family sleeping, claimed that they did not want to sleep in their parents' apartments, and that on those few occasions in which they did so, they were eager to return to the children's house.

negate their influence, or to deny that adaptation to external social and cultural variables may produce a dynamism of its own, it would appear that we must look elsewhere for a more adequate explanation.

## Motivation by psychocultural and psychosocial determinants internal to the actors

When cultural values and norms are internalized by the actors, they constitute motivational dispositions. We may plausibly identify two such "psychocultural" determinants of the sabra counterrevolution. It might be suggested, in the first place, that as girls the sabras internalized the traditional values of their ambivalent mothers. Although intellectually committed to the feminist ideology of the kibbutz, many of the pioneer women nevertheless remained ambivalent about its actualization in the new forms of marriage and the family that they themselves had created. Some of them, for example, chafed at the normative expectation of minimizing the importance of the marriage bond. Others never emotionally accepted the collective rearing of children and the consequent separation from them. Their unmilitant acceptance of the emerging sexual division of labor might be interpreted as still another sign of their ambivalence. It is hard to believe that the ambivalence of these mothers, which was very evident in 1951 (see Spiro 1955:232 ff), was not communicated to their children, resulting in the transmission of some of their persistent traditional values. That, however, these values were internalized by their daughters, or (even if they were internalized) that they comprised the motivational basis for their counterrevolution is equally hard to believe in view of the fact that their sons, who presumably received the same conflicting messages, did not react in the same manner.

But sabra enculturation was (and is) not confined to the kibbutz. A kibbutz, after all, is far from being an isolated community, and insofar as the counterrevolution was brought about by psychocultural determinants, the latter may have consisted in motivational dispositions acquired through the internalization of values extrinsic to the kibbutz. Thus, from early childhood the sabras are exposed both to the larger Israeli society and culture by personal encounters with and experiences in it, as well as to societies and cultures of other times and places by their excellent education in humanistic and social studies. Not surprisingly, therefore, sabra mothers (like their own mothers before them) often inquire why the kibbutz family is different from that found in most of the world. Is it "natural," many of them ask, that they should live apart from their children? These extrinsic cultural influences, it should be added, are importantly augmented in their period of compulsory military service (two years for the females, three for the males) during which the kibbutz system is often challenged by nonkibbutz army peers.

Although it would be rash to deny any influence to these extrinsic cultural values, it is doubtful that their internalization—if, indeed, they have been internalized—was an important determinant of the counterrevolution. For, we must ask, why is it that these extrinsic cultural values were not internalized by and did not similarly motivate the male sabras? Moreover, since most of the social and cultural values of the outside world are different from, and often opposed to, those of the kibbutz, why did they not stimulate a counterrevolution in the other foundations of kibbutz society and culture? Why, for example, have the sabras retained the kibbutz system of collective ownership of the means of production? Why have they maintained its system of radical equality in the distribution of goods and services? Why have they not returned to the profit motive? And so on. In short, why should the values of the outside world have had such a selective influence on the sabras? Indeed, why should their influence have been selective even within the narrow range—marriage, family, and so on—in which it has, putatively, been primary? Thus, for example, in view of the continuing opposition of Israeli women outside the kibbutz to premarital intercourse (Hazleton 1977:132), why have kibbutz women retained the permissive kibbutz attitude to premarital sex, both in theory and in practice?

Since, then, there are serious problems to attaching primary importance to these putative psychocultural determinants of the sabra counterrevolution, let us turn instead to some possible psychosocial (precultural) determinants. The most obvious hypothesis to consider in this connection is the well-known phenomenon of adolescent rebellion and generational conflict. It has been frequently observed, especially in nontraditional societies, that if parents, or the older generation, are committed to one set of values and institutions, their children (as a form of rebellion) often acquire an opposite set. Since, then, the kibbutz pioneers accomplished a revolution in the traditional values concerning the family and sex-role differentiation, their daughters' counterrevolution might be interpreted as an instance of this psychological process of adolescent or generational revolt against adult values.

There are at least three difficulties, however, with this explanation. First, if their counterrevolution was motivated by rebellious needs, it should have spent its course by the time the sabras attained maturity. We have seen, however, that they persist in these changes even as mature adults. Second, if it were merely a generational phenomenon, then the daughters of the first-generation sabras should have rebelled in turn against their mothers' counterrevolution, thus restoring the system to its status quo ante. On the contrary, however, these changes have now persisted into the second generation sabras. Third, even for the first generation, their counterrevolution, as we have seen, did not consist so much in changing the revolutionary institutions established by their mothers—for it was the latter who had already brought about many of the changes—as in celebrating those that had already occurred, and advancing them even further.

In sum, it seems that we can assign little more importance to these possible psychocultural and psychosocial determinants of the counterrevolution than to the possible sociocultural determinants discussed in the previous section. Still, we cannot adequately judge their importance until we assess them relative to the importance of still other possible determinants. To do this, we must attend to a set of data which we have heretofore neglected—the behavior of the sabras as children. Since the counterrevolution occurred in the first instance among the first cohort of females to have been born and raised in the kibbutz (when its feminist ideology was triumphant and its revolutionary changes in marriage, the family, and, to a somewhat lesser extent, the sexual division of labor were firmly established), many of the conditions comprising these three sets of possible determinants were simply not present. Hence, for this cohort, at least, an adequate explanation of the counterrevolution requires an examination of their childhood as well as their adult behavior. Unfortunately, there are no data from any kibbutz on the childhood behavior of this cohort. We do have data, however, at least from Kiryat Yedidim, on the childhood behavior of the cohort who were children in 1951, and it is their behavior that I now wish to examine.

## Sabra childhood

In 1951 there was a total population of forty-seven preschool children in Kiryat Yedidim—those who had passed out of the infants' house but had not yet entered kindergarten. Ranging in age from thirteen months to exactly five years, these forty-seven children were distributed in four ascending age-graded children's houses. Since, however, one of these houses contained only one male (which renders sexual comparisons in that group rather tenuous), it has been excluded from our discussion, leaving a total population of forty-one children. Old enough to talk, run, and play games, yet young enough so that their effective learning environment was pretty much confined to the children's house, it is this population of twenty-two boys and nineteen girls whose behavior we shall describe and compare. Since at any given time the system of "collective socialization" (*chinuch meshutaf*) is fairly uniform across all kibbutzim, these children, though representing only one kibbutz, can be taken as a more or less random sample of those sabras who grew up in mature kibbutzim in that period in their history.

In that period, to be sure, the feminist ideology and institutions of the kibbutz were no longer present in pure form. However, since the early fifties represent the watershed between the revolutionary and counterrevolutionary periods of kibbutz history, it is probably fair to say that this is the last cohort of sabras whose behavior as children might assist us to disentangle the childhood from the adult determinants of the counterrevolution. Thus, although many of the possible sociocultural determinants discussed in the previous sections were already present, insofar as most of them relate to adult experience, any assessment of their influence on this cohort of sabras depends on the extent to which their childhood behavior exhibited signs of the counterrevolutionary behavior that they now display as adults. Before examining their behavior, however, we must briefly describe their learning environment.

Raised jointly from birth, these children spent most of their lives in their respective children's houses, except for a daily two-hour visit to their parents' apartments. Based on the kibbutz belief in the "identity" meaning of sexual equality, the social environment in the children's houses (beginning with the infants' house) was explicitly structured to minimize sexual differences in behavior and experience. In each house boys and girls played, slept, ate, and showered together, and (during their toilet training) sat on their training pots together. As far as possible, the socialization of both sexes was the same. Moreover, boys and girls shared the same toys, and all play and games taught them by the nursery teachers were sexually integrated and undifferentiated. The same pattern characterized their other learning experiences. Boys and girls alike were inculcated with the same values concerning the importance of agriculture and labor. They worked together in the "children's farm," comprising a vegetable garden, some sheep, and a poultry run. Their responsibilities within the children's houses were also undifferentiated and nonsegregated. In short, except for differences in dress and in personal names, no observable sexual differences were inculcated in the children by the personnel in the children's houses (their most important learning environment) either by instruction or by the social reinforcement (approval, rewards, etc.) of sexually differentiated behavior. The children's experiences in their two-hour visit with their parents were little different. Except for the fact that babies were nursed by mothers, mothers and fathers displayed one parental role, rather than differentiated "paternal" and "maternal" roles. Not surprisingly, therefore, when in 1951 we elicited descriptions of the socialization roles of their parents from these children, they described only minor differences between father and mother.

On the basis of this summary description—for a detailed description, see Spiro (1958:chs. 2–9)—it seems reasonable to conclude that so far as this was possible the learning environment of these children was highly similar for both boys and girls. Since this is no longer true today—for with the counterrevolution, socialization in the kibbutz no longer follows this pattern of radical sexual uniformity—the behavior of these children might provide an important clue to the determinants of the sabra counterrevolution. For if sex differences in motivation are culturally acquired, we would expect children raised in this kind of learning environment to have displayed few if any sexual differences in behavior. Hence, if they did display such differences, it is likely that they were motivated more by precultural than by culturally acquired needs. If, moreover, there were important correspondences between their childhood and their subsequent adult behavior, such that the sexual differences found in their adult behavior can be seen to have been prefigured in their child-hood, it would then be likely that their counterrevolution was moti-vated more by sex differences in precultural determinants than by the cultural determinants discussed at the beginning of the chapter. Let us then turn to the childhood behavior of these sabras, paying particular attention to possible sexual differences. We shall begin with free play, their most frequent type of behavior.

*Free play.* In the course of our observations in the children's houses in 1951, each of the 41 children comprising our sample was ob-served in a mean number of 24 play sequences, for a total of 997 separate sequences comprising 56 different types of free play. Too large for meaningful comparisons, these types in turn were further broken down into a small set of structurally based categories induc-tively arrived at. It is these categories which comprise the basis for the sexual comparisons summarized in Table 1. Although the mean-ing of some of these categories is obvious, others require a brief ex-planation.

Each children's house contained a large variety of toys and other play materials that were shared by and were freely available to all the children. Since, however, the category, "toys," is much too em-bracing, it has been broken down into two subcategories in Table 1. "Microscopic" toys are small toys and other play materials that are used by being held in the hand, while "macroscopic" toys are those which are climbed on, driven, and so on. In addition to toys, each children's house contained a sandbox in its play yard; and play with sand was combined with play with other natural objects, such as mud, stones, and tree branches, to form one structural category, "sand and natural objects."

But not all play consists of play with objects. The category, "verbal and visual" play consists of singing, chattering, looking at picture books, and storytelling. "Locomotor" play consists of running, jump-ing, gymnastics, and so on. "Fantasy" play refers to imaginary activi-ties in which the child pretends to be (identifies with) some person or thing, and enacts the behavior or role appropriate to the object identified with. Thus, pretending to be a dog, the child gets down on all fours "barking" at and biting the other children. The use of the term *fantasy* does not imply that fantasizing did not occur in the other play categories; sometimes, for example, a child driving a tricycle would pretend to be driving a car. The distinguishing criteria, therefore, were whether or not the fantasy depended on the use of toys or other props, and whether or not the child was imitating or identifying with the model.

Turning now to our findings, it can be seen from Table 1 that there

Table 1. A comparison, by sex, of structural categories in the play of preschool children in Kibbutz Kiryat Yedidim.

| category | boys | girls |
|---|---|---|
| toys | 41% | 30% |
| microscopic | 24 | 21 |
| macroscopic | 17 | 9 |
| locomotor | 16 | 12 |
| sand and natural objects | 16 | 14 |
| fantasy | 14 | 20 |
| verbal and visual | 10 | 19 |
| miscellaneous | 3 | 5 |

Note—$x^2=20.04$; $d.f.=5$; $p=<.01$.

are important sex differences in the structural categories of play preferred by these children. In the first place, although all toys were freely available to both boys and girls, the boys preferred to play with toys much more frequently than girls did. It will be noticed, moreover, that the main difference consists in the use of macroscopic toys, which the boys preferred by a margin of almost 2 to 1 over the girls. Similar sexual differences are found in those categories of play that do not consist in the use of toys. Thus, boys exceeded girls in locomotor play, while girls exceeded boys in fantasy, as well as in verbal and visual play.

Locomotor play and play with macroscopic toys both consist of strenuous, muscular activity, and when these categories are combined we see that this dimension of behavior is one that boys rather than girls preferred by a wide margin (33 to 21 percent). Similarly, fantasy and verbal and visual play might also be said to exhibit a single dimension of behavior, and the girls' preference for this—the artistic-imaginative—dimension was clearly much stronger than the boys' (39 to 24 percent). When boys and girls are compared on these two dimensions the results indicate even more clearly that muscular-physical activity is a male dimension, while artistic-imaginative activity is a female dimension of play. (By the $X^2$ test, the difference is significant at the .001 level.)

These dichotomous dimensions can be viewed as reflecting behavioral orientations that might be variously designated (depending on one's theoretical perspective) as mechanical-artistic, active-passive, realistic-intuitive, concrete-imaginative, and any number of others. But however they are designated, these findings clearly indicate that even as preschool children the sabras exhibited important sex differences in behavior, the significance of which for this study is obvious. If, according to received cultural interpretations, sexual differences in behavior are determined by culture, how are we to explain these important differences between the play of boys and girls who (as we have seen) were raised in the same learning environment, whose socialization had been uniform, who had been taught the same play and games, and whose socializers (parents and nursery teachers) were committed to the abolition of sex differences in behavior? Since, in this kind of cultural regime, it would be unlikely for these differences to have been culturally determined, it is much more likely that they were determined by precultural motivational differences between the sexes. If so, whatever the correspondences in their details, we would expect to find some disposition to sex-role differentiation in the adult behavior of the sabras as a function of these precultural sex differences in their motivational orientations as children. Although the categories and dimensions used in this first classification of free play are too general and abstract to point to detailed correspondences of this kind, the men's greater preference for physical labor is certainly one example. If, then, a closer analysis of sex differences in their play might establish even closer correspondences between the childhood and adult behavior of the sabras, such a finding would pose a serious challenge to a cultural interpretation of the counterrevolution. This being the case, it is all the more important that this challenge be scrutinized in some detail.

According to cultural interpretations, sex differences in motivation are acquired as a function of the acquisition of those cultural values which, varying from society to society, define (and ultimately determine) the appropriate behavior for each sex. Since sex differences in behavior are exhibited by young children, these values must be acquired very early, and, according to cultural theorists, they are acquired by imitating sexually appropriate "role models." In general, anthropologists have not been interested in the mechanisms underlying sexually appropriate role modeling. Relegating these mechanisms to "psychology," for anthropologists it has been enough to observe that, whatever these mechanisms might be, this is the process by which children come to internalize the cultural values which govern sexually appropriate behavior. But this explanation, of course, only pushes the problem one step back, for if, ex hypothesi, there are no precultural sex differences in motivation, how do children come to prefer same-sex models in the first place? Psychologists, at least those who agree that these preferences are culturally determined, have proposed various theories to account for the mechanisms underlying sex-role modeling. Here, I shall examine only the two most prominent—social learning theory and cognitive theory.

According to social learning theory (Mischel 1966), children's preference for same-sex role models is acquired by the process of "social reinforcement." Since, prior to the acquisition of their cultural values, children of both sexes indiscriminately exhibit similar forms of behavior, and since adults are very much concerned that they behave in a culturally appropriate fashion, the latter offer children "positive" reinforcement (praise, approval, material rewards) when their behavior corresponds to that of same-sex models, and "negative" reinforcement (ridicule, disapproval, punishment) when it corresponds to that of cross-sex models. As a consequence children acquire a preference for sexually appropriate models, and by imitating them they learn those types of behavior that, in their society, are culturally appropriate for their sex.

According to cognitive theorists (Kohlberg 1966), social reinforcement is not necessary for the imitation of sexually appropriate models. Regardless of reinforcement, children begin to imitate same-sex models when they reach that stage of cognitive development at which they can make judgments concerning their gender identity. Once this cognitive judgment is achieved, then, assisted by their perception of the sex-role differentiation found in their social field, the cognitive foundation for sex differences in imitation has been prepared. Based on a postulated need to value those things that are like the self, boys (having judged themselves to be male) value masculine things, and girls (having judged themselves to be female) value feminine things. Hence, boys (valuing masculinity) are motivated to imitate male models, and girls (valuing femininity) are motivated to imitate female models.

In short, both cognitive and social learning theory agree that sexual differences in children's behavior are ultimately determined by variable cultural values which in different societies require different forms of behavior from each sex; they agree too that these values are acquired by the imitation of sexually appropriate adult models. For social learning theory, however, the imitation of same-sex models is motivated by the learned desire for the positive reinforcement that accompanies the performance of culturally appropriate behavior, while for cognitive theory, their imitation is motivated by the innate need to value those things that are like the self. Despite their differences, however, both theories agree that prior to the acquisition of these cultural values, there are no sex differences in motivation. Hence, sex differences in behavior must be a function of the imitation of sexually appropriate role models, and sex preferences in role models must be culturally acquired.

Despite the distinguished pedigrees of these cultural interpretations, neither explains the sex differences exhibited in the free play of our sample of sabra children. In the first place, it is unlikely that these sex differences in our findings could have been determined by sex differences in the behavior of adult models. That the boys preferred play with toys and locomotor play and the girls fantasy and verbal and visual play surely cannot be accounted for by sex differences in adult behavior, for in the narrow sense none of these categories corresponded to the behavior of adults of either sex, and in the broadest sense they all corresponded to the behavior of adults of both sexes.

But even granting that these sex differences in play were determined by sex differences in the behavior of adult models, it is unlikely that the children's motivation can be accounted for by the motives postulated either by social learning or cognitive theory for sexually appropriate imitation. For girls to have exhibited a greater preference than boys for fantasy play, for example, it is necessary, according to social learning theory, for girls to have been more strongly reinforced than boys for fantasy behavior. It is most unlikely, however, for this to have occurred, for given their belief in the "identity" meaning of sexual equality, kibbutz socializers in 1951 were intent on discouraging the development of sex differences in these children. Hence, in the entire year in which we observed child socialization, we seldom observed any type of social reinforcement of child play that might expectably have led to sex differences in motivation. If, moreover, the social reinforcement model is applied to the dichotomous behavioral dimensions which we extracted from the children's play, this critique applies even more strongly. In 1951, in order to achieve their conception of sexual equality, kibbutz socializers would not have differentially encouraged those activities in boys which exhibited a muscular-physical dimension and those activities in girls which exhibited an artistic-imaginative dimension.

Nor does cognitive theory, according to which children's imitation of sexually appropriate models is motivated by a need to value the behavior of adults of the same gender, fare any better. For to the extent that the categories of sabra play corresponded to adult behavior, the correspondence (as I have already noted) was with the behavior of adults of both sexes. Hence, rather than exhibiting sexual preferences in their free play, boys and girls should have been randomly distributed across all play categories. When cognitive theory is applied to the sex differences in the dichotomous behavioral dimensions we extracted from sabra play, the force of this critique is even stronger. The early fifties, as I have already indicated, comprised the watershed between the feminist revolution and the feminine counterrevolution in the kibbutz. At that time, therefore, many women were still working in farming and other physically strenuous activities. Nevertheless, although children of both sexes had sexually appropriate models for the muscular-physical dimension of behavior, the latter was a preferred dimension in the boys' but not in the girls' play.

In short, contrary to cultural interpretations, this analysis suggests that it is unlikely that the sex differences exhibited by sabra children in their free play could have been determined by the sex differences in the behavior of adult models; but even on the assumption that they were, it is even more unlikely that the motivation for their imitation could have been determined either by social reinforcement or by the need to value things like the self. It might be objected, however, that this conclusion is unwarranted because by the structural classification of play described above it is not possible to assess the cultural determinants of sex difference in motivation. Cultural determinants might be said to relate more to the content of behavior than to the formal or structural dimensions which comprise the basis for this classification. In order to deal with this objection, let us then turn to an analysis of the content of the children's free play. In undertaking this analysis, I shall treat fantasy and other forms of play separately since the former has two distinctive properties that are specifically related to the question of imitation: its content is based (by definition) on the imitation of role models, and in enacting these roles, the children pretend to be (identify with) these models.

*Fantasy play.* For our present purpose the most significant finding to emerge from a content analysis of fantasy play consists of the different preferences of boys and girls respectively in their choice of role models. As Table 2 indicates, the most frequent role enacted by

*Table 2.* A comparison, by sex, of role models in the fantasy play of preschool children in Kibbutz Kiryat Yedidim.

| role model | boys | girls |
|---|---|---|
| animal | 48% | 23% |
| adult female | 26 | 47 |
| adult male | 16 | 13 |
| baby or younger child | 8 | 15 |
| inanimate object | 2 | 2 |

Note—$X^2=13.24$; $d.f.=4$; $p=<.01$. This table is taken from Spiro 1953: 270.

the girls ("adult female"), comprising almost half of their fantasy play (47 percent), was that of a parenting woman (mother, child caretaker, nursery teacher), while the most frequent role enacted by the boys, also comprising almost half of their fantasy play (48 percent), was that of an animal. From our description of the kibbutz in 1951, and of the learning environment of these children at that time, it is highly unlikely that these sex differences could have been determined by the processes described either by cognitive or social learning theory. Let us begin with the latter.

According to social learning theory, it will be recalled, sex preferences in role models are determined by the social reinforcement of sexually appropriate behavior, as a consequence of which children acquire a preference for imitating the behavior of same-sex models. As I have already emphasized, during the period in which we studied kibbutz children, kibbutz socializers refrained from administering those social reinforcements that might expectedly lead to sex pref-

erences in behavior. Of course, it would be absurd to deny categorically that some degree of reinforcement did not take place; after all,
however strong their commitment to the "identity" meaning of sexual
equality, the kibbutz pioneers were themselves the products of a traditional cultural system, and (as I have previously mentioned) their
traditional values concerning sexually appropriate behavior had not
entirely disappeared just because they had become radical feminists.
Indeed, in 1951, believing that sex differences are culturally determined, I assumed that our observations were insufficiently sensitive
to discern those subtle cues in the behavior of socializers which,
though often missed by outside observers, are nevertheless perceived
by children. Hence, although in a previous analysis of these sex
differences in the fantasy play of sabra children (Spiro 1958: chaps.
8–10), I primarily adopted a cognitive interpretation, I simply took
it for granted that these differences (as well as the others summarized
in Table 2) were also the consequence of persisting traditional values
of kibbutz socializers who transmitted them by subtle techniques of
social reinforcement. A second, and harder, look at these findings
makes it evident, however, that this is an invalid interpretation; for
even if this were true, social learning theory nevertheless leaves most
of the findings concerning sex differences in the fantasy play of sabra
children unexplained.

We shall begin with the girls' choice of parenting women as their
preferred models because, insofar as it bears upon our understanding
of the counterrevolution, this is the most important finding of our
study of sabra fantasy play. For brevity, I use "parenting women" as
a collective term to designate mother, child caretaker (*metapelet*),
and nursery teacher (*ganenet*), and I shall likewise use "maternal
roles" as the collective term to designate their respective roles.
(These terms are descriptively accurate not only because the behavior of all three women is properly characterized as "parenting,"
but also because in most societies their roles are viewed as "maternal"
inasmuch as they are performed either by the mother alone or by
mother surrogates. In the kibbutz, the child caretaker and nursery
teacher were explicitly conceived as mother surrogates who would relieve mothers of many of their traditional maternal responsibilities.)

Now, even assuming, in accordance with social learning theory,
that the girls' preference for female models was determined by subtle
reinforcement techniques which we did not discern, why is it that of

all the female roles found in the kibbutz at that time, the girls chose maternal roles exclusively? In 1951, the kibbutz system of sex-role differentiation being fairly fluid, many women were still working in the vegetable gardens, dairy, vineyards, and fruit orchards, not to mention the kitchen, laundry, and sewing room. The girls were aware of this diversity of nonmaternal female roles not only because many of their own mothers performed them, but also because in their daily hikes through the kibbutz they frequently observed many other women in nonmaternal roles. Hence, even on the assumption that girls chose adult female over adult male models by a ratio of almost 4:1 (47 to 13 percent) because kibbutz socializers, still tied to notions of sex-role differentiation, reinforced the girls' imitation of female models only, we are still left with the question of why, among the many female models available to them, they chose to imitate maternal models exclusively. Moreover, even on the unlikely assumption that kibbutz socializers were even more traditional than their parents and only reinforced the girls' imitation of maternal roles, the girls nevertheless should have imitated at least some of the other female models since, according to social learning theory, reinforcement of sexually appropriate behavior leads (by stimulus generalization) to a preference for other roles performed by same-sex models.

Other findings concerning fantasy play likewise constitute a critical challenge to a social learning interpretation of the girls' preference for maternal roles. For if this preference is explained by the hypothesis of social reinforcement, then, if kibbutz socializers reinforced the culturally valued choices of the girls, they would hardly have refrained from reinforcing the culturally valued choices of the boys. Hence, just as girls displayed a preference for female (and specifically maternal) models, we would expect the boys to have displayed a preference for male models. Despite this expectation, however, rather than choosing adult males, the boys chose animals as their preferred models, and by a margin of 3 to 1 (48 to 16 percent) over adult males. Would we then seriously wish to argue (in accordance with social learning theory) that the imitation of animal behavior, being deemed culturally more appropriate than men's behavior by kibbutz socializers, was more vigorously reinforced? Or that boys chose animal models twice as often as the girls (48 to 23 percent) because their socializers, believing that animal-like behavior was culturally more appropriate for males than for females, offered boys and girls differential reinforcement?

Although we shall raise still other challenges to a social learning interpretation of the girls' preference for parenting women, I first want to assess this finding in terms of cognitive theory. The latter, because of an important structural feature of the learning environment in the children's houses, seems to be less vulnerable to this challenge. According to cognitive theory, it will be recalled, children imitate the behavior of same-sex models because, having a need to value things like the self, once they achieve cognitive awareness of their gender identity, girls value feminine and boys value masculine things. Since, then, the entire personnel in the children's houses was female, it could be argued that in their need to value things like themselves girls chose parenting women exclusively as female role models because they were the cognitively most salient females in the learning environment in which they spent most of their time. This same variable—cognitive salience—might also explain the boys' infrequent choice of men models: since there were no males among the personnel in the children's houses, men were not as cognitively prominent for the boys as women were for the girls.

Although seemingly persuasive, this interpretation is critically challenged by the other findings concerning the children's fantasy play. For if cognitive salience explains both the girls' choice of parenting women as their preferred models and the boys' infrequent choice of any men models, how then are we to explain the boys' choice of animals as their preferred models? If only because of the prominent role of fathers in their lives, men were surely no less prominent in the boys' cognitive field than animals, and yet they not only preferred animal to adult male models by a margin of 3:1, but they chose them almost as frequently (48 percent) as all their other models combined. Moreover, the animals with which the boys identified did not comprise the cognitively salient domestic species encountered either in their daily chores on their miniature farm (lambs and chicks) or on their daily hike through the kibbutz (sheep, cows, and chickens), but they comprised such infrequently encountered species as snakes, dogs, wolves, and horses. If, then, the variable of cognitive salience does not explain the preferred models of the boys, we cannot invoke it to explain those of the girls—unless, of course, we wish to postulate cognitive salience as a sex-linked factor in imitative behavior. Short of adopting the latter hypothesis, we can only conclude that some factor other than cognitive salience accounts for the girls' choice of parenting women and the boys' choice of animals as the preferred models of fantasy play.

Cognitive salience aside, the boys' preference for animal models poses still other challenges to a cognitive interpretation. Thus, for example, would we seriously wish to claim (in accordance with cognitive theory) that once they established their masculine identity, the boys greatly preferred animal to men models because kibbutz values more significantly associated masculinity with animal than with men's behavior? Or that their preference was motivated by the postulated need to value things like the self?

And what about the children's cross-sex identifications? If (according to cognitive theory) the establishment of gender identity leads to the imitation of sexually appropriate models, why did the boys choose adult females much more frequently than adult males as models (26 to 16 percent)? And why did the girls choose male models only slightly less often than the boys did (13 to 16 percent)?

These latter findings, of course, are as challenging to social learning as to cognitive theory. Moreover, both are equally vulnerable to the challenge from the final sexual difference exhibited in the children's fantasy play. As Table 2 reveals, girls identified with babies and younger children twice as often as boys (15 to 8 percent). Would we then say, following social learning theory, that this difference is to be explained by the assumption that kibbutz socializers, deeming infantile behavior to be more appropriate for girls, reinforced the girls' choice of these models more vigorously than they did for boys? Or would we say, following cognitive theory, that by kibbutz values infantile behavior was a better way of maximizing femininity than masculinity?

In sum, from this analysis it seems highly unlikely that the sex differences displayed by sabra children in their fantasy play could have been culturally determined inasmuch as neither the culturally inappropriate preference of the boys (animals) nor the culturally appropriate preference of the girls (parenting women) can be explained by either of the two theories of role modeling. Hence, rather than being motivated by culturally acquired needs, it seems more likely that these sex differences were motivated by precultural needs.

As we shall see, this interpretation can account not only for the girls' choice of parenting women as their preferred role models, but also for the boys' preference for animals. Moreover, it can also account for the other preferences summarized in Table 2 which, being either sexually or culturally inappropriate, appear to be anomalous from a cultural interpretation. I shall begin with the girls' preference.

On the assumption that sex preferences in children's choice of role models are motivated by differences in precultural needs (whether in degree or in kind), it follows that boys and girls, respectively, should prefer those models whose behavior is viewed as a means for gratifying those needs. By this theory, parenting women may be said to have been the preferred role models of sabra girls because the imitation of their maternal roles served to gratify the girls' own parenting need. (Whether this precultural need—if such it is—is to be taken as innate, or whether it is to be taken as socially, but nevertheless preculturally acquired, will be discussed below.) Now, cognitive theory holds, it will be recalled, that the choice of role models is motivated by one and the same precultural need. Having established their distinctive gender identities, it is the innate need to value things that are like the self which, according to this theory, motivates children to choose models of their own gender. That in the present case the establishment of a feminine identity was a prior condition for the preference of sabra girls for female models is highly likely—after all, their preferred models were female, not male. But that, of all the female models available to them, the girls chose parenting females exclusively suggests that this preference was motivated not by a need to value that which the self is like—femininity—but by a need to value that which the self wishes to be like—a parent. In other words, this finding suggests that the girls were motivated to prefer these particular female models not because they were like them—clearly, with respect to their distinctive features of parenting, they were not—but because of a wish to become like them.[2] That the frequency with which the girls chose

2. There is abundant evidence to support the hypothesis that adults, as well as children, choose their models from social categories that possess attributes which they desire, and that, motivated by this desire, they emulate or identify with these models in order to become like them. This phenomenon is alluded to by social psychology in the distinction between levels of achievement and of aspiration, by sociology in the distinction between membership and reference groups, by psychoanalysis in the distinction between ego and ego ideal, and so on.

maternal models almost equalled that of all their other choices combined further suggests that the parenting need was the most powerful of all their needs.

Contrary, then, to cultural interpretations, this analysis suggests that sex differences in children's choices of role models can be determined by precultural needs, and that a preference even for culturally appropriate models need not be culturally determined. This does not imply, however, that culture is merely an epiphenomenon, or that cultural theories of role modeling have no explanatory value whatsoever. For, as these data indicate, if a culturally appropriate model is chosen, the children's behavior complies with the culturally prescribed role. For example, although the preference of the sabra girls for maternal models may have been motivated by a precultural need, in identifying with these models they enacted the norms that govern maternal behavior in kibbutz culture. Whether they learned these norms by observing the behavior of these models or, alternatively, because of social reinforcement, is a theoretical issue we need not enter here. In either case, this analysis suggests that cultural theories of sex differences in the role modeling of children are not so much theories of motivation as of cognition: although they do not account for the acquisition of sex preferences in role models, they do account for the acquisition of the cultural norms governing role performance.

If, then, sex preferences in children's choice of role models are motivated by precultural needs, we can account—as cultural theories cannot—for the culturally inappropriate preference of sabra boys. For if the girls' preference for maternal models, though culturally appropriate, is best explained by postulating a precultural parenting need, the boys' preference for culturally inappropriate animal models can only be explained by postulating some other precultural need. In the absence of relevant data, however, we can only speculate about what such a need (or needs) might be.

Animals, as is well known, frequently acquire symbolic meanings, and since the animals with which the boys identified in their fantasy play comprised infrequently encountered species, mostly of the natural environment (horses, dogs, snakes, frogs, and wolves), rather than the frequently encountered domesticated species of their behavioral environment (cows, lambs, sheep, and chickens), it seems reasonable to assume that the former species were indeed chosen for their symbolic significance. Since, moreover, these species were either wild or potentially dangerous, it does not seem entirely rash to assume that they represented (as is often true in dreams and Rorschach responses) either the boys' own aggressive impulses, or those they projected onto others. When we then consider that many of these boys were in the oedipal stage of psychosexual development, aggressive impulses of an oedipal character suggest themselves as specific candidates for consideration. For this is the developmental stage at which boys' identifications with animals may serve the defensive function of disguising their own hostile impulses, or (if the animal symbolically represents the father) of defending themselves against the fear of the father's hostility (realistic or imputed) by the well-known defense of "identification with the aggressor." That, in the present case, their preference for animal models progressively decreased, and was finally replaced by men models as the boys reached the age of five, lends credence to these speculations because, of course, this is the age when typically the Oedipus complex is being resolved, and the need for such defensive maneuvers is obviated. The conjecture that these animals may have had aggressive meanings (oedipal or not) for these boys is supported by findings (to be reported below) on their aggressive behavior outside of fantasy play.

Still, all this is speculative. Hence, whatever the symbolic meaning that animals may have had for these boys I should like to turn to the important theoretical question implicit in their preference for these culturally inappropriate models, namely: what is the implication of the existence of precultural needs (especially if, as in this case, they lead to a preference for culturally inappropriate models) for the functioning of culturally constituted social systems? Although a society can permit such needs to be gratified initially in the enactment of culturally inappropriate roles (especially if, as in this case, it is confined to fantasy play), such forms of gratification cannot be tolerated for long. And it is this problem that explains the pivotal function of socialization (social reinforcement) in the maintenance of social systems—not, however (as social learning theory has it) as a means for the acquisition of culturally appropriate needs, but rather (as I have argued) for the acquisition of cultural norms that ensure the gratification of precultural needs by culturally prescribed means. (This, of course, is what is meant by "sublimation.") Since our kibbutz boys eventually relinquished their preference for animal models in favor of culturally appropriate ones, it can be assumed

that this is exactly what happened to those precultural needs, whatever they may have been, that had been initially gratified in their
enactment of animal roles.

As I have already observed, the boys' preference for animal models
is only one of the findings concerning sabra fantasy play that is
anomalous from the perspective of a cultural theory of role modeling.
Other findings are anomalous, however, not because they are culturally, but because they are sexually inappropriate. Cultural theories
of sex differences in motivation assume that there is an ontogenetic
progression from sexually undifferentiated motives to sexually differentiated (culturally acquired) ones. That the boys, therefore, chose
parenting women as their second most frequent role models (second
only to animals) is one anomaly for cultural theories, as is the fact
that the girls chose men models almost as frequently as the boys did.
These findings, however, pose no anomaly for a precultural interpretation for (as I have stated more than once, and as these findings explicitly demonstrate) sex differences in precultural needs are differences in degree not in kind. Hence, it is not surprising that boys, as
well as girls, should have exhibited a strong parenting need in their
fantasy play. That they initially gratified this need, however, by identification with parenting women—after all, they also had parenting
men models—is a problem that will be taken up below. For the present, we need only observe that this finding (like that concerning the
girls' identification with men) points to the pivotal function of socialization for harnessing precultural needs to culturally appropriate
roles. It is through socialization that boys and girls learn to gratify
their sexually undifferentiated needs by the performance of culturally differentiated sex roles.

Let us now summarize the tentative conclusions suggested by
the sex differences in role modeling found in the sabras' fantasy
play: (a) for a culturally appropriate sex model to be preferred above
all others, it is not necessary (as the girls' preference for parenting
women indicates) that the preference be culturally acquired; (b) that
a model is culturally appropriate is not sufficient for it to be preferred
(as the infrequency with which boys chose men models indicates);
(c) for a model to be preferred, it is not necessary (as the boys' preference for animals shows) that it be culturally appropriate; (d) for
a culturally appropriate model to be chosen at all, it is not necessary
that it be sexually appropriate (as is shown by the identification of

children of both sexes with cross-sex models). Since, then, these conclusions run contrary to cultural interpretations of role modeling, and since even prior to their acquisitions of cultural values governing sexually appropriate behavior, these sabra children manifested important sex differences in their choice of role models, it seems reasonable to suggest that they were motivated by differences between boys and girls in precultural motivational dispositions.

If this is so, then these findings concerning fantasy play provide one important explanation for the counterrevolutionary attitudes of the female sabras toward the family. Since, as children, parenting women comprised their preferred role models, and since this preference seemed to have been motivated by a desire to gratify a precultural need, it is reasonable to assume that the need for parenting was one of their strongest precultural needs. Given, then, that the strong motivation they display in their mothering roles today was already prefigured in their fantasy play in childhood, it seems not unlikely that their counterrevolutionary attitude to the family was determined more by this putative precultural need than by some culturally acquired need, or by cultural conditions to which, as adults, they were required to adapt. An analysis of the children's nonfantasy play not only supports this conclusion, but it also suggests that there was a precultural motivational disposition for other aspects of their counterrevolution as well.

*Nonfantasy play.* Nonfantasy play refers to play and games using toys and other material objects in which (with some exceptions to be noted below) there was no identification with adults, although their behavior may have been imitated by the children. As was indicated above, it is unlikely that the sex differences in the structural dimensions of this type of play were culturally determined. For some of the same reasons, it is not likely that sex differences in its content were culturally determined. First, much of this play, being child-specific, was not based on the imitation of adult models. Moreover, even in those types of play which were based on imitation—driving a toy automobile, for example—it is unlikely that sex preferences were acquired through differential reinforcement since (as has been repeatedly noted) kibbutz socializers attempted to discourage rather than encourage sex differences. There is simply no evidence for the assumption that boys drove toy autos, wagons, and tricycles more frequently than girls because the former were reinforced for imitating culturally appropriate role models.

Similar problems challenge a cognitive interpretation of sex differences in the content of their nonfantasy play. Even assuming that most of this play was based on role modeling, it will be remembered that in 1951 the sexual division of labor in the kibbutz was highly fluid. Hence, if the children of one sex displayed a greater preference for play that corresponded to a role that was performd by adults of both sexes, it could hardly be argued that this sexual preference was motivated by a need to enhance their gender identity.

To be sure, despite this fluidity, there was a great deal of sexual specialization in the kibbutz even at that time. We have already seen, for example, that women did not work with heavy equipment, and that men did not perform traditionally female roles. Even so, however, a cognitive explanation seemed unlikely. Thus, the content of locomotor play (slides, swings, running and jumping games, and so on) and of visual and verbal play could not have been modeled after sexually specialized adult roles, and yet every item comprising the former category was chosen more frequently by boys than by girls, while every item comprising the latter was chosen more frequently by girls than by boys.

What, then, about play with "macroscopic" and "microscopic" toys? In the case of the former, it could be argued (following a cognitive interpretation) that the boys' greater preference for scooters, tricycles, and wagons was determined by the fact that men, but not women, drove trucks, tractors, combines, and so on. If so, how then do we explain the greater preference of the boys for wheelbarrows when, in fact, the adult most frequently observed by the children to work with a wheelbarrow was a female landscape gardener, who worked near and around the children's houses?

With respect to play with microscopic toys, this category comprises three subcategories: mechanical toys (model cars and planes, building blocks, tinker toys, tin cans), art materials (modeling clay, finger paint, crayons), and dolls. Boys chose toys comprising the first subcategory more often than the girls, while girls chose those comprising the latter two more often than the boys. (For all three comparisons the differences were significant, by the critical ratio test, at the .001 level). Although, given the sexual specialization that existed in the kibbutz at that time, it could be argued (by a cognitive interpretation) that the boys' preference for mechanical toys was culturally determined, how then are we to explain the girls' preference for dolls and art materials? For neither case were there specifically female models. As far as art is concerned, there were kibbutz artists of both sexes, and as far as parenting is concerned, the parenting role of the father was just as prominent as that of the mother. For as we have seen, the children spent two hours every day in their parents' apartments, and both parents devoted that period to playing with and caring for them.

In sum, there are at least three reasons why it is unlikely that sex differences in nonfantasy play were culturally determined. First, some of the differences were not based on role modeling, there being no correspondence between certain forms of play and any apparent model. Second, even in those cases in which role modeling was either explicit or inferred (from correspondences between the children's play and adult behavior), the children's preferences were very different from those predicted either by cognitive or by social reinforcement theory. That is, in the 23 percent of the play which was (either explicitly or inferentially) based on role modeling, the models were culturally inappropriate—animals, babies and young children, and inanimate objects—and nevertheless boys and girls exhibited differences in preference. Moreover, when the models were culturally appropriate, the sex differences were often sexually inappropriate; that is, they either did not reflect the distribution of the sexes in the adult sex-role system or, what is a greater difficulty, they sometimes were the reverse of that distribution.

For all these reasons, it seems more reasonable to assume that sex differences in the content of nonfantasy play, like those exhibited in fantasy play, were determined by sex differences in precultural needs. On this assumption we can also explain why it is that these differences were quantitative rather than qualitative. For, as we have already seen, precultural theories assume that the sexes are differentiated not by categorically different needs, but by differences in the relative strength of the same needs.[3]

3. Having empasized the bisexual character of precultural needs, it should at least be noted that not all the differences found in the play of these children were quantitative. In the oldest group in the sample, for example, who ranged in age from 49 months to 5 years, 56 different types of play were recorded, of which 54 percent were performed by both sexes, 25 percent were performed by girls exclusively, and 21 percent by boys exclusively. In short, the overlap be-

What light, then, if any, do these findings shed on the sabra counterrevolution in sex-role differentiation? If the latter had been motivated by precultural needs, we would expect the distribution of the sexes in the present sex-role system to have been prefigured in the sex preferences which, as children, the sabras exhibited in their nonfantasy play. To test for this isomorphism, the content of this play, insofar as it was explicitly or implicitly based on human models, was classified as "adult male" or "adult female" according to its correspondence to sex roles presently found in the kibbutz. The results (as Table 3 demonstrates) indicate that there is indeed a close correspondence. The boys' preferences prefigured present male roles nearly twice as frequently as the girls' (79 percent to 41 percent),

---

*Table 3.* A comparison, by sex, of the isomorphism between the nonfantasy play of preschool children in Kibbutz Kiryat Yedidim and contemporary economic sex roles.

| sex roles | boys | girls |
|-----------|------|-------|
| male | 79% | 41% |
| female | 21 | 59 |

Note—$x^2=8.86$; $d.f.=1$; $p=<.01$.

---

while the girls' prefigured present female roles almost three times as frequently as the boys' (59 percent to 21 percent).

Since then, the shape of the sabra counterrevolution in sex-role differentiation may be said to have been prefigured in the sex differences exhibited in their childhood play, and since it is unlikely that the latter differences were culturally acquired, it seems reasonable to assume that the counterrevolution initiated by the sabras in the sex-role system, like that in the family system, was determined to a large extent by sex differences in precultural motivational dispositions.

*Nonplay behavior.* Having examined the play of the sabras as young children, we may now turn to other aspects of their childhood behavior, where again some clear-cut sex differences seem to prefigure their counterrevolution. These differences do not relate ex-

---

comes especially prominent when specific play events are classified into smaller categories. Within these categories, however, there are differences in kind as well as degree.

plicitly to such relevant variables as parenting because, of course, in "real" behavior (in contrast to fantasy play) preschool children cannot care for babies,[4] but they are found in other relevant variables. Thus, for example, in each of the four children's houses comprising our sample, girls exhibited more "integrative" behavior (aid, assistance, sharing, and cooperation) whereas boys exhibited more conflict and, in three of the four houses, more aggression. Moreover, although boys and girls alike attempted to restrain peer aggression, only the girls were observed to offer consolation to the victims of aggression. These sex differences in aggression, conflict and nurturance clearly parallel the differences between the boys and girls in their preferences for animals and parenting women, respectively, which they exhibited in their fantasy play.

The sex difference in aggression found in these children are especially significant since this difference has been found to obtain across species as well as across cultures. In his survey of mammalian behavior, Gray (1971:30–32) found that males universally are more aggressive than females. Similarly, in a cross-cultural study of children, aged 2 to 6, in 101 societies, Rohner (1976) reports that boys, without exception, were more aggressive than girls. In still another cross-cultural study, Barry (in an unpublished paper cited by Rohner) found the same results for children aged 4 to 6 in a sample of 125 societies. Maccoby and Jacklin, who report the same findings for American children, comment that this sex difference in aggression has been observed "in all cultures in which the relevant behavior has been observed. Boys are more aggressive both physically and verbally. They show the attenuated forms of aggression (mock-fighting, aggressive fantasies) as well as the direct forms more frequently than girls. The sex difference is found as early as social play begins—at age 2 or 2½" (Maccoby and Jacklin 1974:352).

Since Maccoby and Jacklin observe that in the United States this sex difference persists at least through college, and since Barry reports the same result for children from the age of eight to adolescence in a cross-cultural study of 137 societies, it might at least be noted that

4. Such differences, however, seem to have been prefigured in the behavior of a somewhat older cohort. Beginning in kindergarten, for example, girls would often assist their mothers (if the latter were caretakers for younger children) in caring for their charges, while boys only infrequently did so. Moreover, these same girls would assist younger children in feeding and dressing, but this was not true of the boys.

this same result was obtained in the case of kibbutz children. In 1951, in a cross-sectional comparison of children in the grammar school in Kiryat Yedidim, I found that girls exhibited much less aggression than boys. Moreover, they also exhibited much more cooperation and assistance. More than that, in the sixth grade a small group of girls (aided by some few peripheral boys) constituted what might be called the moral leadership of the grammar school, spurring on the other children to accept their responsibilities and to live up to the norms of the school. At that time, at least, this phenomenon occurred with regularity, not only in Kiryat Yedidim but also within the entire kibbutz movement, moving one educational researcher to character-ize it as "almost a law."

If, then, this moral leadership of the girls may be labeled "expres-sive," it is striking that the association of "expressive" and "instrumen-tal" leadership with males and females, respectively—an association which Parsons (1951:79–88) suggested some time ago—was found among these sabra children as early as the age of four. When they reached this age, one child came to initiate most of the group's activi-ties, and that child was invariably a boy. It was to him that the others looked for guidance. According to the nursery teachers, the sexual specificity of this role occurred with such predictable regularity that they had come to refer to its incumbent as the "king" (*melech*) of the group. Typically the strongest boy, the king was turned to by his peers not only for instrumental guidance, but for protection against peer aggression. Although sometimes he too might aggress against his peers, he would nevertheless protect them from the aggression of others.

Now these sex differences in the children's instrumental-expressive leadership patterns and in their aggressive-integrative behavior could hardly have been influenced by differential reinforcement, for con-sistent with kibbutz values boys and girls alike were strongly en-couraged to engage in cooperative and to refrain from aggressive behavior. Similarly, it is unlikely that they were influenced by imita-tion of adult behavior, for among adults physical aggression was practiced by neither sex, and adult leadership roles were beyond the experience of these pre-school children. These differences in child-hood, in short, were most likely based on precultural determinants. This is also the conclusion arrived at by Barry on the basis of his cross-cultural study. Since only 20 percent of the societies in his sample encouraged boys to act more aggressively than girls, that boys were the more aggressive in all societies could not have resulted from sex differences in socialization.

Since, then, these particular sex differences in sabra childhood behavior were most likely determined by differences in precultural needs, insofar as their behavior prefigured certain characteristics of the counterrevolution which they instituted as adults, it seems reasonable to conclude that the latter characteristics were motivated by the same needs. Thus, for example, the counterrevolution in kibbutz governance includes such patterns as women serving as the general secretary, but not as economic manager of the kibbutz, or of women playing a dominant role in educational and welfare committees but not in economic and political committees; and these patterns may be said to have been prefigured in the sex differences in expressive and instrumental leadership which the sabras exhibited in childhood. Similarly, certain aspects of the counterrevolution in sex-role differentiation, including the men's preference for physical and the women's preference for educational occupations, seem to have been prefigured in the marked differences between boys and girls in the strength of their aggressive and integrative needs, respectively.

We may now summarize this chapter. On the assumption that the sabras' behavior as children might shed some light on the counterrevolution they instituted as adults, we examined their behavior as it was observed in 1951 when they were still of preschool age. However their behavior was classified—play and nonplay, as well as fantasy play and nonfantasy play—and by whatever criteria it was analyzed—structural properties and content—there were important and significant differences between boys and girls. This finding pointed to two conclusions. First, since it is unlikely for these sex differences to have been culturally determined, this finding suggests that it is more likely that they were determined by precultural differences between the sexes. Second, insofar as the sex differences in their childhood behavior seem to have prefigured some of the core features of the counterrevolution, this finding further suggests that the latter, too, were primarily motivated by these same sex differences in precultural needs. If these conclusions are valid, the kibbutz experience lends support to the thesis that, contrary to received opinion in the social sciences, many of the sex differences that are universally found in human societies are a consequence not so much of cultural determinants, as of precultural motivational differences between the sexes. Although the particular content of the sex differences found in human family systems, occupational roles, and political behavior is undoubtedly determined by the historical circumstances unique to each society, the universality, as well as the shape of these differences, would seem in large part to be a consequence—so the kibbutz experience suggests—of sex differences in precultural motivational dispositions.

# Chapter 5. Conclusions

## A precultural interpretation

Any attempt to assess the possible determinants of the counterrevolutionary changes that have occurred in the kibbutz movement in such institutions as marriage, the family, and sex-role differentiation is beset with formidable difficulties. The problem is too complex, the data are too limited, and our methods of investigation were too primitive to permit an unequivocal interpretation. The weight of the evidence nevertheless suggests that although the possible cultural determinants discussed at the beginning of the last chapter may have contributed to these changes, on balance they do not appear to have been decisive. Evidence from sabra childhood behavior suggests, instead, that these counterrevolutionary changes were more probably brought about not primarily as a response to external cultural conditions nor by culturally acquired motives, but by precultural motivational dispositions.

Since, however, it is a basic axiom of the social sciences that human behavior and motives are primarily, if not exclusively, culturally programmed, I wish to observe, lest this conclusion be rejected on axiomatic grounds, that the counterrevolutionary changes in the above domains were not the only (nor even the most dramatic) changes brought about by the sabras. A perhaps even more dramatic change occurred in the sexual domain. Hence, before continuing with this discussion, I would like to examine briefly this latter change which constitutes a rather unequivocal exception to our social science axiom.

According to the ideology of the kibbutz pioneers, attitudes and orientations to sexual behavior and sexual anatomy are cultural artifacts. Hence, so they believed, if children were raised in a sexually permissive and enlightened environment, in which boys and girls, living together, were acquainted with each other's bodies and were taught to view nudity as natural, so that notions of shame were not attached to the exposure of sex organs—in such an environment, differences in sexual anatomy would assume little more importance than any other kind of anatomical differences. This belief was important for the pioneers not only because of their commitment to healthy sexual attitudes, but also because of their conviction that sexual equality (in its "identity" meaning) required an attitude of indifference to sexual dimorphism. If, as they believed, the only "natural" difference between the sexes consists in differences in sexual anatomy, if children were raised to view this difference as inconsequential, the road to sexual equality (as they conceived it) would then have been paved.

Acting upon their beliefs the pioneers established an entirely "enlightened" sexual regime in the children's houses. Boys and girls used the same toilets, dressed and undressed in each other's presence, walked about their dormitory rooms (if they chose) in the nude, showered together in one shower room, and so on. This system worked (and works) as the pioneers expected until the first intimations of puberty in the girls—in general, girls enter puberty a year or two before the boys—at which time the very girls who had been raised in a sex-blind environment developed intense feelings of shame at being seen in the nude by the boys. Sometime before our 1951 study, the girls in Kiryat Yedidim, for example, initiated an active rebellion against the mixed showers: they began to shower separately from the boys, refusing to admit them into the shower room at the same time. Consistent with this attitude, some of the girls would return early to their children's house at night to undress and be in their pajamas before the boys arrived.

Despite the girls' active opposition, the educational authorities refused to change the system of mixed showers. Moreover, when high schools were built in the kibbutzim, mixed showers and bedrooms were instituted in the high school dormitories as well. By 1951, however, the mixed showers in most kibbutz high schools had been unofficially abandoned. As one teacher in Kiryat Yedidim put it, the mixed showers had become "a form of torture" for the girls, their shame at exposing their nude bodies in front of the boys being intensified by the latter's teasing. Hence, though the high school authorities did not officially sanction it, arrangements were made for boys and girls to shower at different times. In a survey I conducted in Kiryat Yedidim in 1951, only three students in the entire student body favored a return to the mixed showers. Today, the sexes not only shower separately, but in almost all kibbutz high schools there are now separate shower rooms for boys and girls.

The same process has taken place with respect to the dormitory rooms. I have already noted that even in the grade school the older girls felt considerable discomfort about undressing in the presence of the boys. Their discomfort was exacerbated in the high school. In 1951, for example, although boys and girls in the high school in Kiryat Yedidim shared the same rooms (usually three boys and three girls to a room), they were careful to undress in the dark with their backs to each other. Moreover, so that their bodies would not be exposed, the girls wore pajamas (regardless of the heat) even though they slept under sheets. Despite these precautions, succeeding generations of students have been persistently unhappy with these living arrangements until, seven years ago (and after many generations of female protest), the high school authorities capitulated to the girls' demands, and instituted unisexual bedrooms. Similar changes have been introduced in most other kibbutzim as well.

In sum, the original kibbutz belief, that in the proper learning environment children would be sex-blind, was proven to be false even in the sexually enlightened conditions in which these children were raised. Even if it were the case that the only natural difference between males and females is one of sexual anatomy, this one difference apparently is not as trivial as had been assumed. In this instance, at least, it had important social and psychological consequences which could hardly have been culturally determined, for these children (as we have seen) developed a sense of sexual shame not as a result of, but in opposition to, the cultural values of their learning environment.[1] Apparently, nudity on an impersonal and anonymous

1. In 1951, under the influence of kibbutz ideology, the high school personnel attributed the sabras' reactions to the influence of students from the city who had imbued them with feelings of sexual shame. Being a cultural determinist at that time, I too found this to be a persuasive explanation although, in retrospect, its flaws are obvious. First, these shameful feelings were almost always aroused during (or shortly before) pubescence when most girls, still in the grammar school, were not yet exposed to city students. Second, even for those whose puberty was delayed till high school, the assumption that the cultural values of a tiny minority of outside students could prevail over those of the majority, especially when the latter were natives (supported by the entire weight of their native and much more prestigeful environment) makes little sense. Moreover, if the absence of sexual shame is natural and its acquisition cultural, this explanation makes even less sense, for one would then have expected the cultural to give way to the natural. If the kibbutz students were indeed influenced by the city students, it is more reasonable to believe that they

bathing beach is one thing; but in an intimate and potentially sexually charged small group, it is quite another. When, then, the social institutions that embodied these cultural values became too painful for the children, they pressed for their abolition in violation of the attitudes in which they had been imbued and over the opposition of the adults.[2]

Is this not the same process that describes the counterrevolutionary changes in the family and sex-role differentiation which were instituted by the sabras upon becoming adults? In the case of these children, reared in a learning environment that was predicated on the assumption that sex differences in behavior and psychology are cultural artifacts, that boys and girls differ only by virtue of their sexual anatomy, and that this difference becomes socially important only so far as culture makes it so—in the case of these children the sex differences in behavior that they exhibited very early in their lives were exhibited in spite of and in opposition to their learning environment. This being so, it seems most likely that these sex differences (like their sense of sexual shame) were brought about not by culture, but by the triumph of human nature over culture, that is, by motivational dispositions based on sex differences in precultural, rather than culturally constituted, needs. If, then, the counterrevolution of the female sabras was motivated by precultural needs, these needs cannot be unique to them; rather, all things being equal, it is probable that they are shared by females in any society. Hence, having thus far avoided any discussion of the types of precultural needs that might explain these sex differences in motivation, we must finally address this issue directly.

## Precultural needs and the sabra counterrevolution

In the typology of possible determinants of the sabra counterrevolution outlined on pp. 64 ff., three types of precultural needs were

---

were ready to be influenced because this influence was syntonic with their natural dispositions.

2. It is pertinent to observe here that these children, whose behavior refuted the assumption that the shame aroused by sexual dimorphism is cultural, are the same children who, upon becoming adults, reversed the attempts of the pioneers to minimize the importance of dimorphism by eschewing feminine clothing, jewelry, and cosmetics. Today, as we have seen, female sabras attempt to enhance their feminine appearance by these cultural means, and male sabras obviously approve of these attempts.

distinguished. One type ("biological needs") consists of genetically inherited drives. The other two ("psychosocial" and "psychobiological" needs) consist of experientially acquired wishes and desires. Here, then, we have three types of determinants of sex differences in motivational dispositions which are present prior to (or, as in some cases, independent of) the acquisition of culturally constituted motives. Although the latter two types are experientially acquired, they are no less panhuman than those genetically inherited because the experiences by which they are acquired are dependent either on certain invariant characteristics of the human organism or on those characteristics of human society that are invariant. Since the invariant characteristics of human society (biparental families, group living, socialization systems, and the like) are institutional solutions to adaptive requirements of human beings (the satisfaction of early dependency needs, for example) which they share by virtue of their constituting a common biological species, these needs too are indirectly "psychobiological." From this perspective, then, those precultural needs that are experientially acquired are no less a part of "human nature" than those that are genetically inherited. In the present stage, at least, of human biological and social evolution, both are invariant characteristics of human personality and both constitute panhuman bases for human behavior. (For the most important anthropological statement of this thesis, see La Barre 1954.)

Although precultural needs, then, may be either genetically or experientially acquired, the research strategy employed in this study does not permit us to decide whether the motivational determinants of the sabra counterrevolution—and, therefore, of precultural sex differences in motivation anywhere—are the one or the other. That the counterrevolution was motivated by precultural needs is an interpretation, it will be remembered, that was adopted only after the cultural hypotheses comprising our explanatory paradigm were finally rejected as incompatible with the data. The precultural interpretation was then adopted not only because it was the one remaining hypothesis in the explanatory paradigm but because it was the one interpretation that was compatible with the entire array of data. On the basis of these data, however, there is no way of deciding whether the sex differences in precultural needs that are reflected in the counterrevolution are genetically or experientially acquired. Hence, the only thing we can do is delineate the shape of these competing types of precultural interpretations by offering examples of the more prominent theories which exemplify each type.

To simplify our task, I shall concentrate on only one need for which, according to our analysis of the behavior of sabra children, there are precultural sex differences. For this purpose I have chosen the parenting need because, in one sense, it is the cornerstone of all the changes that comprise the counterrevolution. The aim of the feminist revolution of the pioneers, it will be recalled, was to minimize the woman's involvement in family, and especially in mothering roles because (it was believed) this would maximize her involvement in extrafamilial roles. This, in turn, was expected to lead to the dissolution of sex-role differentiation, and thereby to sexual equality (in its "identity" meaning). Hence, the feminine counterrevolution, as I have often emphasized, is essentially a phenomenon of sabra females, for while the males have persisted in economically traditional male roles, the females have rejected the more "masculine" of the traditional male roles in favor of other kinds. Moreover, to a much larger extent than the males, the females have also reemphasized the very family—and especially parenting—roles which the pioneers had attempted to deemphasize. Since, then, the parenting need (like most other precultural needs) is shared by both sexes, it is with respect to its greater strength in females that examples of alternative types of precultural interpretations will be examined. In the following discussion, then, "the female parenting need" is used as an ellipsis for "the greater strength of the parenting need in females."

According to one prominent example of a biological interpretation, the female parenting need is an instance of those precultural needs which are genetically determined. Phylogenetically inherited, this need is interpreted in the same manner as any other biological characteristic that is the product of biological evolution, namely, by natural selection. Such an interpretation would hold that in the conditions obtaining in the early history of our species, a strong mother-child bond was an adaptive requirement, so that a strong parenting need in women had a selective advantage. Tracing this advantage to the adaptive requirements of the hunting stage of human evolution, this is precisely the interpretation offered by Tiger and Shepher (1975: 274–77) for the female parenting need and, therefore, for the counterrevolution in the orientation of the female sabras to the family.[3]

3. There are, of course, alternative biological interpretations of the female

According to this interpretation, then, the female parenting need is conceptualized as a "biological" need which, phylogenetically inherited, serves as an internal stimulus to behavior.

We now can turn to examples of those theories of the female parenting need according to which this need, though precultural, is experientially acquired. According to one example, the female parenting need is a "psychobiological" need which is acquired as a result of psychological experiences derived from a biological characteristic of the female organism. Specifically, this need is explained as the motivational consequence of the girl's cognitive and emotional reactions attendant upon her psychic awareness of the structure of her reproductive organs. This theory, as most prominently formulated by Erikson (1963:91), anchors many sex-linked needs in what he calls the "ground plan" of the body. Given that boys and girls have a different "ground plan," each is characterized by "a unique quality of [inner] experience." The experience of girls is different from that of boys as a function of (among other things) the "inner space" that characterizes the female reproductive organs. This experience, which is "founded on the preformed functions" of the "future childbearer," provides girls with a motivational disposition for childbearing and hence for parenting. This thesis has been more extensively developed by Bardwick (1971:15). It is because of the girls' creative inner space, so her thesis goes, that "an anticipatory pleasure and rehearsal of future maternity . . . looms large in the girl."

Perhaps the most influential (and controversial) examples of a "psychosocial" interpretation of the female parenting need are those formulated by Freud (1964, ch. 33). For Freud, like Erikson, this need is acquired as a result of experiences related to female sexual anatomy, but since for Freud these experiences are social (consisting in the girl's interaction with significant others), it seems more accurate to say that for him the female parenting need, though precultural, is more a "psychosocial" than a "psychobiological" need.

According to the first of Freud's hypotheses, if the young girl feels

---

parenting need which, departing from classical Darwinian theory, one might mention—parental investment theory, for example (Trivers 1972). I do not discuss this theory here because although our research design does not permit us to decide whether, as a precultural need, the female parenting need is biologically or experientially acquired, this does not hold for this particular biological theory which (for reasons which would require an extensive discussion) does not seem to adequately explain the kibbutz data.

loved by her mother, then, given the dependency need of children, she develops a libidinal attachment to and identifies with her. Since, for the growing girl, the mother's parenting role is her most important characteristic, the girl's identification with her mother is the basis for her desire to emulate that role particularly. To be sure, the earliest identification of the boy is also, and for the same reason, with the mother; and by this explanation of the girls' acquisition of the parenting need, one would expect that boys would acquire a parenting need no less strong. This is exactly what psychoanalytic theorists like Bettleheim (1954) and others have suggested, a suggestion which receives support from the fantasy play of the sabra children in which, it will be recalled, the second most frequent identification of the boys was with parenting women. Nevertheless, the boy's identification with the mother does not persist because, according to these latter theorists, with his discovery of the anatomical differences between the sexes, he realizes that he cannot become like her. For Freud, however, it is not because he cannot become like her, but because his fear of castration leads him to give up his desire to become like her, that is the crucial factor in the boy's disidentification with his mother. On either interpretation, although boys may subsequently come to envy women for their childbearing function, they give up their identification with the mother.

For the girl, on the other hand, the discovery of the anatomical differences between the sexes has a rather different consequence, which leads to Freud's second hypothesis. When the girl makes this discovery, disappointment supercedes her attachment to the mother as the basis for her parenting need. Viewing herself as having been deprived of a penis, the girl develops a strong wish to acquire one. Eventually, however, she must accept the fact that she cannot gratify this wish (just as the boy must accept the fact that he cannot gratify his wish to bear a child). When, then, the girl gives up her wish for a penis, she puts in its place a wish for a child, and the latter wish acquires all the intensity of the former.

The above four theories are among the most prominent examples of precultural interpretations of the female parenting need. Since, in our present state of knowledge, there is no way of assessing their relative merit, we can only say that all of them can account (in principle) for the precultural existence of this need. But even if all four examples were to be disconfirmed, this would not invalidate the conclusion of this study that the female parenting need is precultural. For if the findings reported here are reliable, the disconfirmation of the above examples of precultural interpretations of this need would merely oblige us to search for alternative interpretations.

On the assumption that the female parenting need is a precultural need, we can not only explain the counterrevolutionary attitudes of the female sabras to the family, but we can also explain the vicissitudes of the revolutionary attitudes of their mothers and grandmothers. For on this assumption, when the kibbutz pioneers rejected (and physically abandoned) their biological family of origin, it is entirely understandable (and in hindsight, at least predictable) that they would have created a sociological family to take its place. Thus it is that the kibbutz, as we have seen, became for them a surrogate family, one, however, in which culture took the place of biological kinship as its basis. Moreover, their repressed parenting need—the women's exaggerated expressions of affection for their grandchildren is evidence for its repression and for the subsequent "return of the repressed"—was initially satisfied by the maternal attitudes they displayed to all kibbutz children. In short, although in the early years of the kibbutz few women performed the role of *genitrix*, any could (and many did) perform the role of *mater*.

But a surrogate family can take the emotional place of the biological family only until one's own family of procreation becomes psychologically important; and on the assumption that the female parenting need is precultural, this must inevitably happen unless the initial motive for the repression of this need is transmitted from one generation to the next. In the kibbutz case, the motive for its repression (whatever it may have been) was obviously not transmitted to the second generation, for the sabras have not only established larger biological families than their mothers, but they have also transferred a significant measure of their familial emotions from the sociological family (the kibbutz), which had been the focus of the familial emotions of the kibbutz founders, to the biological family which each has created herself. This is the process, or so at least it seems to me, by which the kibbutz has been transformed from one, undifferentiated child-oriented community to a structurally differentiated community consisting of separate (though integrated) child-oriented families.

But this is not all. Insofar as the female sabras value parenting as a phase-specific role in the life cycle, the gratifications they derive from this "feminine" role obviate the need to strive for status in "masculine" roles. Confident in and valuing their status in the family domain, their desire, however, for sexual equality in extrafamilial domains has in no way diminished, although it has taken a different form from that desired by women who disvalue the maternal role. Instead of seeking "status identity" with men in a system of sex-role uniformity, the sabras seek "status equivalence" in a system of sex-role differentiation. It is all the more significant, therefore, that although many of them have been frustrated in this attempt by the narrow range of occupational opportunities available to women, they have neither abandoned their familistic orientation, nor have they attempted to reinstate the pioneers' "identity" meaning of sexual equality.

These kibbutz findings, if I may be permitted a personal note, forced upon me a kind of Copernican revolution in my own thinking. When I returned to Kiryat Yedidim in 1975, I realized that my understanding of what I thought I had been doing in the kibbutz in 1951 was very different from what I found myself doing in 1975. As a cultural determinist, my aim in studying personality development in Kiryat Yedidim in 1951 was to observe the influence of culture on human nature or, more accurately, to discover how a new culture produces a new human nature. In 1975 I found (against my own intentions) that I was observing the influence of human nature on culture; alternatively, I was observing the resurgence of the old culture (in modern garb) as a function of those elements in human nature that the new culture was unable to change. If this is so, then what is really problematic about the data presented in this book is not the feminine counterrevolution of the sabras, but the feminist revolution of their parents and grandparents. For if, as these data suggest, many of the motivational differences between the sexes are precultural, and if, moreover, these differences are more or less accurately reflected in the system of sex-role differentiation presently found in the kibbutz (and in almost every other human society), then the challenge for scientific inquiry presented by the kibbutz experience is not why the sabras, in their system of sex-role differentiation, conform to "human nature," but why the kibbutz pioneers had attempted to undo it. Since, however, a nonspeculative answer to this question requires historical data which I do not command, and since in any event the question is best answered by a study of contemporary movements in the West that are making the same attempt today, there would be little gain in offering a speculative answer. Instead, I wish to turn to some of the broader issues implicit in the kibbutz experience.

Unlike cultural theories, which attribute sex differences to sexually appropriate role modeling, our analysis of the kibbutz data has suggested that the obverse is closer to the truth; that is, sexually appropriate role modeling is a function of precultural differences between the sexes. Implicit in this difference between cultural and precultural interpretations of the motivational bases for role modeling is an even more important difference with respect to the origin and persistence of systems of sex-role differentiation. Since, according to cultural interpretations, there are no precultural differences between the sexes, it follows that sex-role differentiation is itself culturally determined. Hence, it is just as feasible for social systems to be constructed on (or to evolve into) a "plan" of sex-role uniformity as of sex-role differentiation. According to precultural interpretations, however, the former alternative is not feasible, for the precultural motivational differences between the sexes renders it highly probable that these differences will inevitably be institutionalized in some type of sex-role differentiation.

Of course, the content of any system of sex-role differentiation is culturally constituted, so that such systems can—and many do—become ossified and exploitative. If, then, as a reaction to such a situation, a particular system were to be abolished, it is highly likely, as the kibbutz experience suggests, that another, albeit nonexploitative system, would take its place. For if many sex differences in motivation are precultural, then systems of sex-role differentiation not only create sex differences in motivational dispositions, but they also constitute important institutionalized means for the expression and gratification of these precultural dispositions. Lest I be misunderstood, I should like to make explicit some of the implications of this conclusion.

1. To say that sex-role differentiation is a consequence of sex differences in precultural needs does not imply that all differences in sex roles are a result of these differences; this inference is both theoretically untenable and empirically false. Moreover, to say that the sexes differ in precultural needs, is not to say that they differ in all precultural needs, nor is it to say that they differ only in precultural

needs, for both statements, again, are theoretically untenable and empirically false.

2. To say that sex-role differentiation, as such, has its origin in sex differences in precultural needs is not to say that sex roles are themselves precultural in origin. Any system of sex-role differentiation is a culturally constituted system; that is, it consists of a set of rules and norms which, viewed as cognitive messages, inform social actors of the appropriate behavioral means by which their needs may be gratified. This being so, although the motivation for performing certain sex roles may stem from a desire to gratify needs, their performance is governed by cultural rules and norms.

3. To say that the performance of some sex-roles gratifies precultural needs (among others) does not imply that sex differences in these needs are differences in kind; rather (as the evidence from sabra children demonstrates) they are typically differences in degree. This is especially true of those needs whose expression and gratification are institutionalized in sex-role systems. Hence, the fact that such systems tend to classify social roles categorically as either male or female does not mean that sex differences in precultural needs are categorically different. On the contrary, so far as these needs are concerned, human beings are most probably bisexual. The behavior of sabra children indicates that both sexes share the same needs, the differences between them consisting of differences in the strength of these needs. Nevertheless, although the differences are in degree, rather than in kind, if the sex-role system does not recognize these differences, then, as the kibbutz data suggest, the social actors will eventually change it.

There is, however, another side to this coin. Whether they are genetically or experientially acquired, it often happens that a reversal occurs in the relative strength of precultural needs. Some males, for example, may exhibit an especially strong parenting need, while some females may exhibit a relatively weak one. This being the case, we may expect that in any society there will be a certain percentage of social actors for whom the culturally appropriate sex roles are psychologically inappropriate. If, then, inflexible boundary rules deny these actors access to the complementary set of sex roles found in their society, or if they are not provided with alternative roles, we may also expect that such actors will exhibit psychological dislocations which, in the absence of relevant structural changes, will lead to sociological dislocations.

4. From the last point it follows that, as a principle of social policy, no social role should be barred to any person on the grounds that his or her recruitment is inconsistent with the current system of sex-role differentiation. In short, no individual or group of individuals should be prohibited from achieving sexual equality in the "identity" meaning of equality. If, however, our findings are reliable, attempts to correct the inequities in any particular system of sex-role differentiation should most effectively be addressed to the achievement of sexual equality in its "equivalence" meaning, for it is the latter meaning of equality that is important for most people to achieve. Hence, for any group of individuals to attempt to impose their particular reversal of a panhuman distribution in sex differences upon others is an insult to their basic human dignity. If, moreover, the political or media influence of such a group assures their attempts a measure of success, the ensuing social and psychological dislocations for the larger society can be expected to be as serious as those attendant upon the reverse kind of straightjacketing (except that in the latter case the consequences are felt only by a minority). For if systems of sex-role differentiation, as such, are in large part a function of sex differences in motivational disposition, attempts to convince women that sexual equality, for example, is worthwhile only in the "identity" meaning of equality, and that "feminine" careers—even if they achieve equality in its "equivalence" meaning—are unseemly pursuits imposed on them by a sexist society, may (if successful) deprive them of important sources of human gratification. Moreover, to the extent that some women are persuaded by this ideology, but continue to be motivated by powerful countervailing needs, the resulting inner conflict may lead, as one psychiatric study has shown (Moulton 1977), to painful feelings of guilt and depression.

Single cases prove little; they are primarily useful insofar as they challenge received opinion. The kibbutz case does not prove the existence of precultural sex differencs. Rather, it challenges the current intellectual and political pieties which deny the existence of such differences (just as they deny the existence of other group differences) on the grounds that to be different is ipso facto to be unequal. That individuals and groups must be identical in order to be equal is surely one of the more pernicious dogmas of our time, and the fact that, ironically enough, it has become a liberal dogma does not make it any the less so. Until or unless the kibbutz data are interpreted differently, the kibbutz case constitutes a challenge to this dogma so far as sex differences are concerned. Of course, the strength of this challenge cannot be determined without much more extensive research—especially longitudinal research—in a variety of cultural settings. Until then, prudence suggests that scientific formulations and public policies related to sex differences proceed with caution.

# References Cited

Anonymous
 1969 *Women of Kibbutz Artzi*. Givat Haviva: Institute for Kibbutz Social Research (in Hebrew).
Anonymous
 1971 *Problems in Collective Socialization*. Givat Haviva: Institute for Kibbutz Social Research (in Hebrew).
Anonymous
 1974 *The Women in the Kibbutz*. Givat Haviva: Department of Women, Kibbutz Artzi of Hashomer Hatzair (in Hebrew).
Bardwick, Judith M.
 1971 *Psychology of Women*. New York: Harper and Row.
Berlin, Isaiah
 1958 *Two Aspects of Liberty*. Oxford: Clarendon Press.
Bettleheim, Bruno
 1954 *Symbolic Wounds*, Glencoe: The Free Press.
Blumberg, Rae Lesser
 1974 "Structural Factors Affecting Women's Status: A Cross-Societal Paradigm." Paper presented at the 1974 Meeting of the International Sociological Association.
Erikson, Erik H.
 1963 *Childhood and Society* (second edition). New York: W. W. Norton.
French, John R., and Naphtali Golomb
 1970 "Introduction to Kibbutz Research." *New Outlook* 13:16–25.
Freud, Sigmund
 1964 *New Introductory Lectures on Psychoanalysis* (1933). *The Standard Edition of the Complete Psychological Works of Sigmund Freud*, vol. 22. London: Hogarth Press.
Gray, Jeffrey A.
 1971 "Sex Differences in Emotional Behavior in Mammals Including Man: Endocrine Bases." *Acta Psychologica* 35: 29–46.
Hazleton, Lesley
 1977 *Israeli Women*. New York: Simon and Schuster.
Kanter, Rosabeth Moss
 1976 Review of L. Tiger and J. Shepher, *Women in the Kibbutz*. *Science* 192:662–63.
Kohlberg, Lawrence
 1966 "A Cognitive-Developmental Analysis of Children's Sex-Role

Concepts and Attitudes." In Eleanor E. Maccoby (ed.), *The Development of Sex Differences.* Stanford: Stanford University Press.

La Barre, Weston
1954 *The Human Animal.* Chicago: University of Chicago Press.

Leviatan, Uri
1975 "Work Life for the Older Person on the Kibbutz." Paper presented at the Tenth International Congress of Gerontology.

Maccoby, Eleanor Emmons, and Carol Nagy Jacklin
1974 *The Psychology of Sex Differences.* Stanford: Stanford University Press.

Maimon, Ada
1962 *Women Build a Land.* New York: Herzl Press.

Mischel, Walter
1966 "A Social-learning View of Sex Differences in Behavior." In Eleanor E. Maccoby (ed.), *The Development of Sex Differences.* Stanford: Stanford University Press.

Moulton, Ruth
1977 "Some Effects of the New Feminism." *American Journal of Psychiatry* 134:1–6.

Murdock, George Peter
1949 *Social Structure.* New York: Macmillan.

Neubauer, Peter B.
1965 *Children in Collectives.* Springfield: Charles C. Thomas.

Padan-Eisenstark, Dorit
1975 "Image and Reality: Women's Status in Israel." In Ruby Rohrlich-Leavitt (ed.), *Women Cross-Culturally.* The Hague: Mouton.

Parsons, Talcott
1951 *The Social System.* Glencoe, Ill.: Free Press.

Rabin, A. I.
1968 "Some Sex Differences in the Attitudes of Kibbutz Adolescents." *Israel Annals of Psychiatry* 6:62–69.

Rohner, Ronald P.
1976 "Sex Differences in Aggression." *Ethos* 4:57–72.

Rossi, Alice S.
1977 "A Biosocial Perspective on Parenting." *Daedalus* 106:1–32.

Sacks, Karen
1976 "State Bias and Women's Status." *American Anthropologist* 78:565–69.

Shain, Rochelle
1974 *The Functional Nature of the Sexual Division of Labor on an Israeli Kibbutz.* Ph.D. dissertation, University of California, Berkeley.

Shazar, Rachel Katznelson (ed.)
1975 *The Plough Woman.* New York: Herzl Press.

Spiro, Melford E.

1954 "Is the Family Universal?" *American Anthropologist* 56:839–46.

1955 *Kibbutz: Venture in Utopia.* Cambridge: Harvard University Press (second edition, 1971).

1958 *Children of the Kibbutz.* Cambridge: Harvard University Press (second edition, 1975).

1960 Addendum. In Bell, Norman W., and Ezra F. Vogel (eds.), *A Modern Introduction to the Family.* Glencoe, Ill.: The Free Press.

Talmon-Garber, Yonina

1956 "The Family in Collective Settlements." *Transactions of the Third World Congress of Sociology.* 4:116–26.

1965 "Sex Role Differentiation in an Egalitarian Society." In T. E. Laswell, J. H. Burma, and S. H. Aronson (eds.), *Life in Society,* Glenview, Ill.: Scott Foresman.

Tiger, Lionel, and Joseph Shepher

1975 *Women in the Kibbutz.* New York: Harcourt-Brace-Jovanovich.

Trivers, Robert L.

1972 "Parental Investment and Sexual Selection." In Bernard Campbell (ed.), *Sexual Selection and the Descent of Man 1871–1971.* Chicago: Aldine.

Tsur, Muki

1975 "Women and Family on Kibbutz." *Shdemot* 4:51–59.

# Index